ECONOMIC PLANNING
IN UNDERDEVELOPED AREAS:
GOVERNMENT AND BUSINESS

EDWARD S. MASON

THE MILLAR LECTURES · NUMBER TWO · 1958

FORDHAM UNIVERSITY PRESS · NEW YORK CITY

Mason, Edward Sagendorph, 1899–
   Economic planning in underdeveloped areas: government and
business. New York, Fordham University Press, 1958.

   xii, 87 p. 24 cm. (The Millar lectures, no. 2)

1. Economic policy.   2. Economic development.   I. Title. (Series)

HD82.M3   330.9   58–59763 ‡

Library of Congress

Foreword

ECONOMIC DEVELOPMENT OF the underdeveloped nations is one of the most difficult and intractable problems facing the world in the second half of the twentieth century. Upon its solution largely depends the stability and peace of the world community.

More than two-thirds of the world's population live in underdeveloped areas, define them how you will—countries with an average annual per capita income of less than $100, or countries in which more than 60 percent of the population is engaged in agriculture. The people in these areas are poor, diseased, illiterate. They are underprivileged. Of course, they have been for centuries but there is a big difference now. Now they know they are poor *and* underprivileged. Now, insistently they want something done about it; they demand improvement and quickly.

Many factors have contributed to the economic awakening of the underdeveloped areas. The development of mass media of communication such as radio, movies, newspapers, and magazines allow them to compare their lot with those of people in industrially advanced countries. They are not happy about the comparison. Then, too, many more visitors are coming from the economically advanced countries: some represent foreign firms interested in local investment; some work on government projects; and, not so long ago, in many areas, there were thousands of soldiers from these economically advanced countries.

Another factor aggravating the intensity of the demand for rapid economic improvement is the intense nationalism of many of these countries.

Some have newly won their independence and are anxious to make their mark in the world. They are not satisfied any longer to be hewers of wood and drawers of water—producers of raw materials for the industrial nations. Instead they want the whole panoply of industrial might—the hydroelectric plant, the blast furnace, and the rolling mill. The people, illiterate and politically and economically immature, demand rapid development; and the frustration of this desire contributes importantly to the social and political instability of these areas.

Now the difficulties that confront economic development in the underdeveloped countries are well understood in the United States and the Western world. Economists and other social scientists have pointed out that the social overhead capital and the pre-conditions necessary for development do not exist in many of these areas. There is a lack of roads, railroads, port facilities, and air ports. Power sources are lacking; capital formation is inadequate; the people are illiterate; public health facilities poor. In many underdeveloped areas, social and religious customs and beliefs inhibit economic activity and prevent the development of a business and managerial class. This has led many observers to the conclusion that development—if it does come—will be measured in decades, not years.

There are, however, many things about development that are not so well understood and appreciated in this country. One of these is the role which government should play in the developmental process. It is to this problem that Professor Mason addresses himself in this second series of Moorhouse I. X. Millar Lectures.

Many believe that there is an optimal relation between government and the economy in the process of development; in the United States, many believe the optimal figure to be close to zero. This attitude is a product of our experience with development in Britain, this country, and the Western world generally—experience, incidentally, which is often misunderstood. Professor Mason rejects any unique optimal or ideal role for government in the process of accelerating development. He develops the thesis that the optimal role of government will vary from country to country and from time to time, depending upon the particular complex of economic and social conditions met in each case.

Professor Mason does not believe that the nineteenth-century experience with development in the Western world is relevant to development in the underdeveloped areas today. The nineteenth-century model is too different from conditions in these areas today to serve as a useful guide. He believes that the state—not necessarily by choice but by necessity—will have to play a larger role in the development of many of the underdeveloped areas today than it did in nineteenth-century Britain and in this country.

Professor Mason is not arguing either for or against a major role for government in the process of economic development. As he himself puts it: "In conclusion, let me say that neither this nor the preceding chapters have attempted to present a thesis either for or against government planning of economic development." As an economist, he has found a high rate of development compatible with almost no government planning, as in nineteenth-century Britain; he has also found a high rate of development compatible with a maximum degree of central control, as in the Soviet Union. From the standpoint of development, the optimal role of the government depends upon conditions of time and place.

In developing these lectures, Professor Mason has performed a very useful function. He reminds us that we cannot make the world in our own image. What was economically best for us, is not necessarily best for them. He helps us better understand and appreciate the different policy paths the underdeveloped nations are following in their efforts to achieve improvement. Lastly — and by no means least important — his reflections should help us frame more intelligent and realistic policies, both public and private, in dealing with the problem of development in the underdeveloped areas.

CHARLES J. WALSH
Department of Political Philosophy
and Social Sciences

December, 1958
Fordham University

Prefatory Note

ONE WHO DISCUSSES THE ROLE of government in economic development has a choice between surveying a field that, if both economically advanced and economically underdeveloped countries are included, is very broad indeed or concentrating either on some aspect of government action or the problems of a particular area. The first choice risks superficiality, the second myopia. Since I have been primarily interested in the contrast between the role played by government in early nineteenth-century development and that typically assumed by government in much of the currently underdeveloped world, and in speculating on the reasons therefore, I have perforce chosen to survey the field with all its attendant risks.

One also has a choice between defending a thesis either for or against the roles currently assumed by government and describing a situation. I have no doubt that, at a particular time and place, there may be a relationship of government and business that is optimal with respect to economic development. But this relationship is highly relative. It is relative to various aspects of the culture of an area, to the stage of economic development, to its economic relations with the surrounding world, and to other influences. The fact that I choose to describe and explain rather than to judge does not mean that I have no views. For example, it is my opinion, that in much of Southern Asia and the Middle East governments are impelled by forces largely outside their control to undertake tasks beyond their competence. This may be said to imply a departure from an optimum government-business relationship. But if governments have, in fact, very little choice in the matter, there does not seem to be much that can be done about it. The plain fact is that throughout the underdeveloped world, the pressures for economic development are all but irresistible. A government that fails to seize the levers of economic development, or at least to make the attempt, is probably not long for this world. Unfortunately, the fact that the pressures are nearly irresistible does not mean that growth will everywhere take place.

Chapter One is principally concerned with the contrast between traditional Anglo-Saxon notions of the proper place of government in the process of development and the place as commonly conceived in most underdeveloped countries. Chapter Two considers the relevance and irrelevance of nineteenth-century experience to the situation now confronting those countries. In Chapter Three, I attempt a survey of the case for government initiated expansion, government direction of investment, and government management of economic activities. This case is largely an attack on the efficacy of private enterprise and the free market in early stages of economic development. The case tends to look stronger before one examines the alternative than it does afterwards. Chapter Four is devoted to some aspects of the alternative course of action; that is, of economic planning in South and Southeast Asia.

These chapters in a somewhat shortened form were given as the Moorhouse I. X. Millar lectures at Fordham University in October, 1958. I am deeply grateful to W. T. Hogan, S.J., and to his colleagues in the Department of Political Philosophy and the Social Sciences for their courtesy and assistance. In the preparation of the manuscript I have benefited from the comments of my colleagues, Alexander Gerschenkron, Simon Kuznets, David Bell, and Gustav Papanek. I am also grateful to Edwin A. Quain, S.J., for his expedition and expertise in seeing the manuscript through the Press.

EDWARD S. MASON

Harvard University

Table of Contents

Chapter One

A Survey of the Terrain

I

THE ECONOMIC DEVELOPMENT with which we in the West are intimately familiar has been largely the product of private enterprise. The whole of western Europe, the United States, the British Commonwealth, and such other areas as achieved substantial economic growth during the nineteenth century were, with the possible exception of Japan, predominantly free enterprise economies. True, the role of government in the promotion of development was larger than is sometimes supposed. And, of course, the relation of government to business varied considerably from country to country. Government action, for example, was much more prominent in Germany and France than in Britain at similar stages of development. Furthermore, everywhere in the Western world the economic importance of government as measured by the relative share of national income generated in the public sector, and in various other ways, has tended to increase. We shall examine some aspects of this nineteenth-century development in the next chapter. Here it is sufficient to emphasize that our close experience of economic growth induces us to assign an overwhelmingly important role to private initiative.

Furthermore, the economic and political ideas that we Americans in particular have absorbed from grade school on have tended to justify this observed relationship. It is useless within the limited time at our disposal to attempt to inquire into the question whether the philosophy of natural liberty was the product or the origin of the economic order that began to unfold so rapidly in Britain towards the end of the eighteenth century. No doubt ideas and events were in complex interaction. But whatever may have been the main direction of influence, it is a fact that this philosophy, of which classical economics was an offshoot, offered a reasoned and, to the contemporary public, a largely satisfactory justification of the existing roles of government in the process of economic growth. This justification, moreover, at least in the economic thought of Anglo-Saxon countries, has remained surprisingly constant over the last one hundred and fifty years.

In 1776 Adam Smith considered the state to have three main functions: defence, the maintenance of law and order, and thirdly, "the duty of erecting and maintaining certain public works and certain public institutions which can never be for the interest of any individual or small number of individuals, to erect or maintain." Keynes used very similar language in proclaiming the "end of Laissez-faire," one hundred and fifty years later. "The most important Agenda of the State," he said, using a Benthamite phrase, "relate not to those activities which private individuals are already fulfilling, but to those functions which fall outside the sphere of the individual, to those decisions which are made by no one if the state does not make them. The important thing for Government is not to do the things which individuals are doing already, and to do them a little better or worse; but to do those things which at present are not done at all."

As Lionel Robbins, who in commenting on these two statements, observes, "The formal similarity is not an accident; it indicates the essential similarity of thought."[1]

It is probably fair to say that the very large increase in the economic role of government between the time of Smith and that of Keynes is the result not so much of a shift in ideas concerning the proper relations of government and business as it is of a change in the nature of the problems that government and business have been called upon to solve. Speaking very generally, the dominant body of economic thought from Smith to Keynes has pretty consistently supported the propositions that the main justification of an economy and its constituent institutions lies in its capacity to satisfy consumer wants for goods and services; that so long as these wants can be satisfied by privately organized business enterprise, that is the proper role for private enterprise; and that, consequently, the economic role of government should be pretty much limited to the meeting of those needs and wants that cannot be met by private initiative. The dominant view has been: let us render unto government only what belongs to government, and let us render unto business the principal task of satis-fying economic wants. And at all stages of development a fairly strong consensus has existed on what in fact belongs to government and what belongs to business.

The fact that the character of this consensus has changed over time is the result mainly of enormous changes in the complexity and wealth of the economy, and, consequently, in the nature of the community's needs and wants. What a complex and wealthy community wants can to a much less extent be satisfied by private enterprise. Industrialization with the at-tendant growth of cities, the expansion of the transportation and com-munications network, the shift from a predominantly self-employed to a predominantly wage- and salary-earning labor force, expanding demands for public health and educational sources, and increasing pressure in our natural resource endowment have all greatly expanded the category of needs that only government can satisfy. But there is little evidence that this increasing role of government has been accompanied by any substantial shift away from the central proposition that those wants that can be satis-fied by private initiative should be so satisfied. If Adam Smith were to survey the current scene, he would, I suspect, find it relatively easy to embrace the observed activities of government within his general princi-ples. The "creep" toward socialism has been much more the product of objective change than of change in ideology.

We are, then, fairly deeply imbued with the notion that there is a proper role for government and a proper role for business in meeting the needs of the community, including the desire for economic growth. And, despite the encroachments of welfare state concepts and the currently heavy demands for national security, the share of the national income represented by the receipts or expenditures of government—federal, state, and local—runs about twenty-five percent; in Britain the corresponding figure would be a little higher. The share of government in capital formation is much less than this. With respect to the business of producing goods and services for sale on the market, the direct participation of government remains negli-gible in the United States. In this area, public action is limited to the pro-vision of rules in accordance with which private action is presumed to serve the public interest.

Even though we have been conditioned by our experience and by re-ceived doctrine to regard this kind of relationship as optimal, we are all probably ready to admit that this optimum is optimal only with respect to a particular historical context. A change in the locus and organization of political power, in the interests of those in power, in the stage of economic development, in the efficiency of the public administrative machinery, and in forms of business organization—to mention no other considerations—can change the relationship between government and business that can reasonably be regarded as optimal. It may well be true that there are certain tasks which, under almost all known circumstances, can be better achieved under private than public auspices; for example, retail trade, cottage industries, and certain types of agriculture. On the other hand, there are certain tasks, the maintenance of law and order, for example, that are normally everywhere performed, and probably best performed, by government.

But almost everything that is done by private enterprise in a capitalist society can be and, on occasion, has been done by government. Currently the role assigned to private enterprise in Soviet Russia is a small one. And conversely, almost everything that is customarily done by government can be and has been done by business. The British East India Company, for over two centuries, was the government of a large part of what is now India. During the last years of the Bao Dai régime in Indo-China the maintenance of law and order in Saigon was turned over to one of the quasi-religious, quasi-criminal gangs that also, as a business enterprise, held the principal vice concessions in the city. It is obvious that government and business are somewhat fluid concepts. If we are to talk about an optimum relationship between government and business, we had better limit the discussion to a particular time and place.

Despite the fact that, as I venture to believe, we would all be willing, at least in certain degree, to admit the claims of historical relativity, it is difficult not to assume that a dispensation that has served us well will not serve equally well elsewhere. That is one of the reasons why the relations of government to business is a subject so close to the heart of devout dogmatists. Regardless of their position in the political spectrum they are as one on the proposition that—regardless of time, space, and history—there is a proper role for government and a proper role for business, from which to depart to any substantial degree is to court disaster. Naturally enough, these extreme views carry over to the problems of underdeveloped countries now seeking economic growth. There are eminent economists and business men in this country who sincerely hold that our foreign aid program will check rather than promote growth in the recipient countries, since aid typically flows mainly through public channels. On the other hand, if we may quote an observation by D. R. Gadkil, one of India's eminent economists: "Today, it is only a very rich country like the United States of America which can afford to talk of free enterprise and even indulge in it and yet not suffer economically." [2]

Not only in India but elsewhere in Southern Asia, particularly in a civil service educated in a strong socialist tradition, the ideology of public intervention runs strong. Christopher Rand draws, in *The New Yorker*, an amusing—but also somewhat depressing—picture of New Delhi at the end of the day when hordes of government clerks, each with his copy of the *New Statesman* strapped to the handlebars, peddle vigorously home from the office.

The vigor with which these divergent views are held is at least moderately surprising since even casual observation of the current scene indicates little or no correlation between the extent of government intervention and the rate of economic growth. In western Europe the "miracle of Germany," allegedly accomplished mainly through the freeing of private enterprise, exists side by side with the remarkable economic growth of Norway's "planned economy." Western Europe as a whole—whose governments exhibit more concern with the economy than is thought proper on this side of the Atlantic—has experienced since the war a rate of growth of national incomes somewhat more rapid than has been achieved in the United States and Canada. In Latin America, where among all the underdeveloped countries of the non-Communist world, reliance on private enterprise is strongest, some remarkably rapid rates of growth, as in Mexico and Colombia, border economies in relative stagnation. In Southern Asia which, since independence, has accorded an enthusiastic reception to national planning, the relative success of India is balanced by the failure of Burma, Indonesia, and Ceylon to regain as yet even the pre-war standard of per capita incomes. The situation is even further confused by the mixed picture presented on the other side of the Iron Curtain.

Reflexion on the recent history of economic development in various parts of the world suggests that a substantial measure of government participation in the economy is compatible both with development and with stagnation. Strong doubts emerge concerning the existence of an optimum relationship between government and business—a relationship that is invariant to the stage of economic development, to the traditions of public and private management, and to the underlying social and cultural institutions of the countries in question. A strategy of economic development suitable to Puerto Rico might fail miserably in Burma, and the role assigned to government in the development of Iraq may be quite inappropriate for Peru. There seem to be more things in heaven and earth than are dreamed of in either the liberal or the planning philosophy. In the words of President McKinley what appears to confront us is "not a theory but a condition."

II

When we turn to an examination of the situation in countries now under-developed but actively seeking economic growth and ask whether the economic role of government is greater or less than would be expected on the basis of the history of Western development, a series of difficulties confront us. How far back in the history of the West would we have to go in order to find a comparable stage of development, if, indeed, it is reason-able to attempt a comparison? What currently underdeveloped areas are we to compare with the early stages of what countries now economically advanced? As we shall discuss in the next chapter, the countries of Western economic development, although all were predominantly free enterprise economies, yet exhibit rather striking differences in the roles assumed by government. And, of course, the differences among countries now under-developed are equally as great. In general, for example, the countries of Latin America tend to place greater reliance on the developmental efforts of private enterprise than do those of Southern Asia. Finally, how are we to compare the relative importance of public as against private economic action at different times and places in view of the tremendous variety of governmental-business relationships that the last two centuries has ex-perienced?

If we consider an underdeveloped country to be one with a per capita income of less than, say $100.00 or (alternately following Kuznets) an economy more than 60 percent of whose labor force is employed in agri-culture, it is clear that, on balance, Western economies in their pre-industrial stage were substantially in advance of the stage at which the underdeveloped areas now find themselves. Britain, the United States, France, and Germany in 1800 enjoyed per capita incomes several times as high as the per capita incomes now current in most of South Asia and the Middle East, in much of Latin America, and in practically all of Africa south of the Sahara and north of the Union of South Africa. Furthermore, as Kuznets points out, the countries of western Europe were, even in their pre-industrial stage, "near positions of economic leadership, and had al-ready experienced a long period of growth and expansion under conditions of political independence."[3]

These countries were already possessed of fairly highly integrated market economies and were, for the most part, politically and socially cohesive national states. They had all experienced the intellectual and moral ferment of the Renaissance and Reformation, they were centers of the scientific revolution that ante-dated the industrial revolution, and their populations were relatively literate.

By comparison, the economies of the countries which, on my definition, are now underdeveloped, are economically primitive. All this has a bearing on the significance of one of the possible measures of the relative importance of the economic role of government; that is, the share of government in the national income. While the share of governments of underdeveloped countries in national income may be roughly similar to that which governments of currently advanced countries had in their pre-industrial stage, it is typically very much less than current shares in these advanced countries. In countries with per capita incomes of less than $100.00, the share of government runs customarily from 6 or 7 to about 15 percent. In Western countries with per capita incomes of, say $800.00 and above, the figure customarily varies between 20 and 30 percent. In non-Communist countries there is a rough correlation between per capita incomes and the share of government in national product.[4]

The principal reasons for this are not far to seek. Low incomes ordinarily mean even lower taxable capacity. Since, for the mass of the population, incomes barely reach subsistence levels, there is not much for government to lay its hands on. Furthermore, although income inequalities are usually very large in underdeveloped countries, administrative inexperience and, frequently, the location of political power, palsy the hand of the tax collector in his approach to large income receivers. Secondly, these countries being underdeveloped, have relatively primitive minimum requirements for government. The 60 percent or more of the population in agriculture is quite largely in subsistence farming. As the example of Indonesia perhaps indicates, life goes on, and the relatively unintegrated economy continues to function, after a fashion, regardless of what happens in government.

Measures of the distribution of wealth, employment, and value added tell the same story. Since even nonagricultural activities lie predominantly in the areas of small-scale enterprise—wholesale and retail trade, cottage industry, and local construction—the share of existing wealth, value added, and employment in the private sector is overwhelmingly large. These facts are important, and they may even suggest to some people that, since the existing distribution of economic activity is overwhelmingly private, governments interested in development might do better by attempting to provide a favorable environment for private enterprise, than by building up the public sector. But do these figures on the existing public and private share in income, employment, and wealth give an accurate picture of the current role typically assumed by governments in the promotion of economic growth in the underdeveloped world? I do not think they do.

An examination of the distribution between public and private channels of new investment, rather than the value of existing investments, gives us quite a different story. In Mexico, where growth has been exceedingly rapid over the last two decades, public investment accounted for 38 percent of total investment in 1939 and reached 45 percent in 1950.[5] The Indian Second Five Year Plan anticipates a governmental share of more than 50 percent of total investment during the period of the Plan. In Pakistan public investment has accounted for roughly two-thirds of the total during the last three years. Figures are lacking on the relative importance of public investment during the early stages of western development, but the available evidence indicates that it nearly everywhere fell far short of typical shares in currently underdeveloped countries.

The role of government in the economy is, moreover, imperfectly suggested by these figures on investment. Public action designed to accelerate and shape the character of development assumes a wide variety of forms throughout the underdeveloped areas of the world. It may be useful at this point, both for an understanding of current practices and for a comparison of these practices with those current at a similar stage in the development of Western countries, to attempt a rough classification of the principal areas in which public action can and does impinge on economic growth.

Although we begin by assuming that government performs its elementary function of maintaining law and order, a word needs to be said about this assumption. It is now fashionable, particularly in Southern Asia, to unfavorably contrast "mere" law-and-order government with the more exalted role public authority is called upon to perform in the promotion of economic growth. In fact, in many countries the greatest contribution that government can make to development is the establishment of law and order. This is certainly true at present in Indonesia and, to a less extent, in Burma. In all probability, a large percent of the remarkable increase in output that has been achieved in China since the Communists took over is properly attributed to the substitution for chaos of something resembling public order. To this extent at least, China's economic progress could have been achieved by any government capable of maintaining internal peace, without the benefit of five-year plans or other manifestations of public concern for economic growth.

The maintenance of law and order, of course, presupposes something more than the ability to take effective police action. It presupposes a government that to some substantial extent rests on the consent of the governed and a society that is something more than a collection of people living within a specified territory. The degree of social cohesion and of political consent that are necessary to the effective maintenance of law and order are usually treated as preconditions of economic growth, and I shall so consider them here. But it is necessary to emphasize that, in certain countries now clamoring for economic development, these preconditions have not yet been fulfilled.

Assuming, however, the effective maintenance of internal security, what are the principal areas in which governments can and do act in the interests of economic growth? One possible classification, to which I shall return in the third chapter, distinguishes measures concerned with expansion of resources, from those concerned with the allocation and management of resources. Resources available to the community can be expanded by increasing the rate of capital formation, through the education and training of the labor force and the maintenance of its health, the bringing into use of natural resources, and the stimulation of entrepreneurship and innovation. The allocation of resources to different uses can be affected by direct government investment, by attention to those institutions necessary to the effective operation of the free market, and by limiting and controlling the operations of the market. The management of resources can be undertaken by government or left to private hands under varying conditions of public intervention.

Direct governmental action typically goes much further in all three areas in currently underdeveloped countries than was characteristic of early Western economic development. Or rather, to speak more exactly, it attempts to do so. In considering this subject, it is well to bear in mind the admonition of the great Swedish economic historian, Eli Heckscher—that there is usually a wide gulf between what in fact happens and what government intends to happen.[6]

In Western economic development, the traditional view held that the key to the expansion of resource use lay in the accumulation of capital and that the overwhelmingly important source of accumulation was the reinvestment of private profits. It followed that the most significant role of government in promoting the expansion of resource use lay in improving the environment for private profit. In Ricardian economics this meant, most importantly, moderating the increase in money wages by an import policy that held down the price of foodstuffs. To be sure, the role of government in promoting the expansion of resource availability was not limited to these measures. The accumulation of capital was facilitated by government action to improve the money market, though frequently this action merely recognized institutional arrangements already initiated by private enterprise. Clearly also, educational and public health facilities made a large contribution to resource availability. But in general, the role of government in resource expansion in the early history of Western economic development lay mainly in providing a favorable environment for private capital formation.

The governments of most of the presently underdeveloped areas are not content with this role. As we have seen, public investment typically accounts for a large fraction of total investment. The contribution of government to the savings process does not, it is true, match its activities as investor. Although it is widely asserted in underdeveloped areas that an acceleration of the rate of capital formation requires a heavy increase in taxation, most government investment is financed by borrowing either at home or abroad and with or without inflation. But it is not only capital formation that engages the attention of governments concerned with expanding resource availability. The five-year plans that dot the landscape of the underdeveloped world typically contain extensive surveys of the human and physical resources available for development and are loaded with recommendations for their increase.

The contrast between the place of government in present economic development and its position in the early development of Western countries is even sharper when we turn to the field of resource allocation. Apart from the provision of that social and overhead capital which private enterprise could not be expected to undertake, early nineteenth-century governments saw their function as mainly the strengthening of those institutions necessary to the functioning of the free market. Resources were allocated principally through private initiative in response to changes in relative prices. In the presently underdeveloped world not only is social and economic overhead capital more broadly conceived than in the early development of the West, but direct public investment is by no means limited to this sphere. Furthermore, the allocative effects of government action in the private sector are not limited merely—or indeed mainly—to improving the functioning of free markets; but to a considerable extent they look toward the undoing or correcting of what would otherwise be the results of free-market operations. The instrumentalities of public intervention are legion: the reservation of certain areas exclusively to government, subsidies, differential taxation, price controls, export taxes and subsidies, exchange controls, quantitative import controls, and a host of others. The combination of these measures varies from country to country, but they proliferate in most underdeveloped areas to an extent unknown in early nineteenth-century development. The problem of resource allocation is, of course, central to the task of development planning; few self-respecting countries in the underdeveloped world, particularly in Southern Asia and the Middle East, feel it possible to get along without their two-to-ten year plans. We shall have occasion to consider later whether these plans are anything more than paper. But to the extent that they bear some relation to reality, they serve to indicate the difference in the area of resource allocation between current and early notions of the appropriate place of government in promoting economic development.

It is conceivable that government could go rather far in attempting to expand resource availability and in controlling resource allocation without undertaking the responsibility of business management. Governments could raise capital primarily to lend to private enterprise; functions now performed by public agencies could be contracted to business; government could control the allocation of resources by limitations on and inducements to private action, rather than by public ownership and operation. In fact, governments in the underdeveloped world have gone much further in the area of public management than was customary in Western development. Japanese economic development was characterized by public ownership and management of enterprises that were later turned over to private hands. Ostensibly the same pattern is being followed in Turkey, Iran, Pakistan, and elsewhere, though it remains to be seen how extensively those enterprises now operated by government agencies will be transferred to private use. But whether the practice is temporary, as it may be in some countries, or permanent, as it undoubtedly will be in others, contemporary governments tend to proceed much further in the field of management than was customary in early Western development.

Contemporary economic development policy, then, assigns an important role to government in all three areas—resource expansion, resource allocation, and resource management. But it is necessary, in order to obtain a fair picture of the relationship of government to private enterprise in the underdeveloped world to draw a distinction between the present as shaped by the past and the present as a hoped-for spring board to the future. And, in considering the emerging future, it is probably wise to distinguish plans from reality. Present underdeveloped areas, as shaped by the past, are overwhelmingly private enterprise economies. The public share in income, wealth, and employment is small. And large areas of economic activity are almost entirely locally independent and relatively untouched by the hand of central government. On the other hand, in those countries actively seeking development—and this is almost the whole of the underdeveloped world—government tends to be the principal agent of development. Not only is the share of government in total investment large, but public action tends to impinge on the development process at many points. But finally, we would do well to recognize that there is frequently a large gap between what the government is trying to do and what in fact gets done. Even in India, which is further advanced in planning than most, the private sector seems to have a way of "overfulfilling" its part of planned growth, while the public sector lags behind. The gap between what gets done and what government is expected to do is even greater. Van der Kroef, the Dutch scholar, draws a picture of expectations in Indonesia which is only a slight exaggeration as applied to some other areas in Southern Asia:

"Especially for the . . . younger generation for whom the colonial era is a dim childhood memory, the state and service to it represent the focal point of youthful ideals and enthusiasms. Revolutionary nationalism has endowed the state with an almost charismatic character, with which the younger generation in particular has identified all its inspirations. In consequence, the improvement of individual or mass is seen as a state function; hence the intense, idealistic interest of even the very young in politics. Independent of the omnipotent all regulating state, welfare and progress are held to be difficult, if not impossible, to achieve."[7]

III

A survey of recent experience in underdeveloped countries leads one then, I think unavoidably, to the view that the role attempted by government and considered appropriate for government, is large. Even in Puerto Rico, which probably relies more heavily on private investment than almost any other underdeveloped area—in this case largely foreign private investment

—development, in the words of a recent historian, "is sparked and guided by government."[8] Indeed, the government of Puerto Rico not only undertakes to provide adequate social overhead facilities, but frequently builds and finances plants, and, through the activities of an effective planning agency, ferrets out economic opportunities.

The appropriateness of the responsibilities undertaken by government in underdeveloped countries is rarely questioned by public opinion in these countries. Indeed, the pressure of opinion is usually in the direction of accelerating and expanding public action deemed necessary to the achievement of a rapid rate of growth. To what extent is this role, assigned to government by popular consent, the product of a climate of opinion, an "ideology," that is markedly different from the climate of opinion in the early nineteenth century? To what extent is this role the product of objective differences in conditions relating to growth? Certainly the differences in ideology are frequently striking. Among the "demonstration effects" of the West that impress an observer in many underdeveloped countries is the prevalence of the demand for social services of all sorts. According to one authority, "Most [underdeveloped] countries want the blessings of the welfare state today, complete with old age pensions, unemployment insurance, family allowances, health insurance, forty-hour week, and all the trimmings."[9]

On the one hand then, Democracy—at least some form of democracy—has preceded the industrialization of most currently underdeveloped areas, while in many of the advanced countries of the West, the diffusion of political power came later in the growth process. The leaders of this emergent, and frequently illiterate, democracy commonly espouse a local and not-too-well defined version of what in India is called a "socialist pattern of society." There are, on the other hand, reasons, entirely apart from ideological considerations, for believing that the conditions relating to growth in the currently underdeveloped areas favor a substantially more extensive participation by government than was characteristic of nineteenth century development. I shall be concerned with some of these conditions and differences in the second and third chapters.

What needs to be emphasized here is that if there can be said to be an optimal relation of government and business with respect to economic development, that relationship is rather different in most underdeveloped areas than it was in the pre-industrial stage of nineteenth-century development. Admittedly, the task of disentangling such an optimal relationship from ideological considerations is difficult, and it probably becomes impossible if ideology is broadly defined. What I want to suggest, however, is that even if the masses and their leaders in underdeveloped areas were not imbued by vaguely socialist ideals and welfare state attitudes but were single-mindedly seeking development by whatever means seemed best, the case for active government intervention would still be stronger than in the early development of the West.

Although there are large differences among countries in the underdeveloped world, and although there were also large differences among the now advanced countries in their pre-industrial stage, certain broad distinctions that bear on the appropriate role of government in the development process are discernible. By and large, as I have already suggested, the countries of the presently underdeveloped world are in certain critical ways substantially behind as compared to the now advanced countries immediately prior to their rapid industrialization. A comparison of stages of development then and now is, to be sure, a tricky business. In some respects, certain currently underdeveloped countries are in advance of certain presently developed countries in the early nineteenth century. But, in those respects which might be considered to facilitate a growth process depending primarily on private initiative most of the underdeveloped world lag far behind. Per capita real incomes are lower; the ratio of savings to national income tends to be lower; the market oriented monetized sector of the economy is frequently smaller; most of the underdeveloped world is more illiterate and probably less permeated by economic rationality than was western Europe and the United States around 1800; geographical and social mobility are probably less. Yet, some of the countries that are furthest behind in these respects have, largely as a result of colonialism, a governmental service stronger in many respects than any of the advanced countries possessed early in the nineteenth century. There are often well-developed transport and communications systems and a limited economic sector in which modern techniques, organization, and methods of management are dominant. This disparity between primitive and advanced elements in underdeveloped societies has a bearing on the role of government in a development program.

Secondly, the presently underdeveloped world is surrounded by countries in an advanced stage of development. The contrast between developed and underdeveloped economies was much less striking early in the nineteenth century. The existence of this juxtaposition has a two-fold significance. A highly productive technology principally adapted to large-scale organization is available for the borrowing. And the tremendous discrepancy in per capita incomes creates in the underdeveloped world, an irresistible pressure for development. Both considerations, as we shall see in a later chapter, tend to favor strong governmental action.[10]

Thirdly, nineteenth-century development took place within a world in which differences in culture (in the anthropological sense) were nowhere near as striking as the differences between most of the underdeveloped and the developed world at the present time. Immigrants moved rather easily into societies not too different from their own, bringing with them capital and technical skills that contributed greatly to the development of the recipient countries. This kind of migration obviously continues to have a sizeable impact on the rate and character of development of many Latin American countries. Elsewhere in the underdeveloped world the transfer of technology will have to take place principally through other channels.

Fourthly, the West's impact during the nineteenth century on most of the underdeveloped world has succeeded in producing almost everywhere an antipathy to private enterprise and, particularly, to foreign private enterprise. The extent of this antipathy varies, of course, among countries; and in some places it may not, over the long-run, seriously affect the course of economic development. Elsewhere, however, the image of the large-scale plantation or industrial organization directed by a hated minority and "exploiting" the mass of unskilled native labor is deeply etched in public consciousness.

Fifthly, the "demonstration effect" of government directed development in the Soviet Union, China, and less recently in Japan is not to be ignored. In the early nineteenth century there were no examples of an association of authoritarian government with economic progress. In fact, government authority was synonymous with stagnation. The inferences now being drawn, particularly in Southern Asia, are frequently quite different.

Finally, the sources of funds available for current development differ substantially from the sources available in the early nineteenth century and, on the whole, this difference favors public as against private investment. In part, the reasons lie in the lower per capita incomes, lower savings ratios, and the primitive state of capital markets in the underdeveloped world. In part, they lie in a shift in the sources of foreign capital supply.

No doubt there are other considerations that would need to be taken into account in an exhaustive treatment of the changing role of government in the development process. What I seek to emphasize is the relativity of this role. It is clearly relevant to the stage of development of the country in question, the state of development of the surrounding world, the receptivity of the culture to private entrepreneurial activities, the administrative competence of government, the sources of developmental funds, and the urgency of popular demands for economic growth. I shall have occasion in the next chapter to consider some of these factors in relation to nineteenth-century growth. In the third chapter I propose to examine some of the economic considerations that are said to favor a dominant role for government in the presently underdeveloped world.

IV

So far I have talked about the underdeveloped world as if the problems confronting the countries making up this world were very similar. There are important similarities, but there are also sharp differences, and it seems advisable, in concluding this chapter, to say something about the differences. Various attempts have been made to classify underdeveloped areas, but none of them seem to be well suited to our purposes. One of the recent attempts to group underdeveloped countries in different classes distinguishes between countries that are densely populated in relation to resources from those that are not; between countries whose growth has been relatively independent and those heavily dependent on outside areas; and between countries whose growth has been largely induced by government and whose growth has been autonomous; that is, the product of private initiative. This leads to a classification of growth processes as Expansionist *versus* intrinsic, Independent *versus* satellistic, Induced *versus* autonomous. [11]

This is a suggestive classification, and an attempt has been made by a Social Science Research Conference to apply it to the growth experience of some ten or twelve countries. [12] This grouping, however, treats as given a distinction that is our concern to explain. And while the relative economic independence of a country and its relation of population to resources no doubt has something to do with the place of government action in economic development, there are probably more important influences. A country that is small in area is likely to be highly dependent on foreign trade. [13] This factor, in the case of Israel, leads A. P. Lerner to the view that unless private enterprise is given a relatively free hand to innovate and produce for the foreign market, Israel will face indefinitely an insolvable balance of payments problem. [14] The greater dependence on foreign trade of the Soviet's European satellites than of the Soviet Union itself may be one of the reasons why detailed government direction of resource use has apparently not worked so well in, say, Poland or Yugoslavia, as in Russia.

If to smallness of territory is added density of population in relation to resources, we have a country that is not only likely to be dependent on foreign trade but one in which economic growth is apt to rely extensively on technique, organization, adaptability, and other human factors. This would appear to reinforce the case for a relatively free hand for private enterprise; and Switzerland may provide a good example. I have no doubt that there are other physical and territorial considerations relevant to the relation of government to business, but the principal influences would appear to be historical and cultural.

Historical and cultural influences tend to have a geographical orientation and consequently, for our purposes, I am inclined to divide the underdeveloped world into geographical regions. Latin America, Africa south of the Sahara and north of the Union of South Africa, the Middle East, and South and Southeast Asia not only embrace most of the underdeveloped world but represent cultural differences that have influenced and will continue to influence the relation of government and business in the process of economic growth. To be sure, physical as well as cultural differences need to be taken into account.

The underdeveloped countries of Latin America in general are rich in natural resources in relation to the population. This significant man-land ratio, to use an oversimplification, has undoubtedly influenced governmental business relationships in many ways, but two are of obvious significance. Large, sparsely settled land areas have presented requirements for overhead facilities, particularly transportation and communications—requirements similar to those presented by the development of the American West—that, in this day and age, only government is prepared to satisfy. The rather large share of public in total investment in a number of developing Latin American countries is mainly accounted for by these sizeable overhead requirements. Secondly, the richness of the resource base has presented large opportunities for private investment, both foreign and domestic, in the production of raw materials and foodstuffs for export. Latin America continues to present favorable opportunities for private investment; and this will undoubtedly, in the future, as it has in the past, have a sizeable impact on the relation of government to business.

The historical and cultural context, however, seems to be even more important. Latin American countries have, for over a century, enjoyed political independence. And if this independence has not brought particularly stable governments or efficient public services, it has at least produced states in which relatively homogeneous populations occupy relatively fixed territories. Into these territories have flooded millions of Europeans, not as colonial administrators but as settlers bringing with them Western techniques and the habits and outlook of Western capitalism. As in all underdeveloped areas at the present stage, the role of government in Latin American development will probably be large, but not as overshadowing as it promises to be in certain other regions.

The African area is by far the most primitive of the underdeveloped world both economically and politically. Even in those countries that have achieved political independence the majority of the population is still tribally organized; and the social, economic, and political institutions that have generally been assumed in the West to be the pre-conditions of economic growth are still to be created. Almost all the development that has occurred to date has come about through foreign initiative and, as Barbara Ward has pointed out: "There is no continent where economic advance depends more absolutely upon outside resources and where the main levers of modernization lie, in the immediate future at least, more exclusively in other people's hands."[15]

Since the war, something on the order of ten billion dollars in foreign capital has been invested in this area. But, unless these countries, whether nominally independent or not, are to remain enclaves of foreign private capital, a very large volume of capital and technical assistance will have to flow through public channels. Indigenous development depends heavily, in the immediate future, on the creation of social and economic overhead facilities—education, public health, the establishment and maintenance of law and order, transportation and communications, an agricultural advisory service, and the like. This is not likely to come about without extensive foreign public assistance.

The Middle East is difficult to characterize in a discussion of conditions and prospects of development, though quite clearly there are factors that distinguish this region from other parts of the underdeveloped world. Egypt is confronted by a population problem that is not shared by the other countries of the area, with the possible exception of Lebanon. Turkey enjoys a degree of political stability and of economic development that, although far below western European standards, is yet far above most of the rest of the area. Israel is *sui generis*. In the rest of the Middle East, including Iran, the dominant factors relating to development appear to be the possession of oil revenues that represent a prodigious potential, a degree of political backwardness and instability that is unique in the world, and a scarcity of private entrepreneurship that borders on complete absence.

Iran and Iraq are putting their oil revenues to effective use, but the social and political changes that normally precede or accompany development have not yet put in an appearance. Saudi Arabia, rushing madly from the eleventh into the twelfth century, has found other uses for oil revenues. None of these countries possesses a stable government, and with respect to none, with the possible exception of Iran, can it be said that the geographical boundaries are stable. Governments and frontiers will undoubtedly change many times before the social and political conditions of sustained economic growth have been established. Private entrepreneurship, where it can be said to exist at all, is pretty much limited to agriculture, trade, money changing, and local construction. For all these reasons it seems probable that if and when a sustained process of development is put in motion, government will play a dominant role. But it takes a hardy forecaster to chart the probable path of economic development in the Middle East.

South and Southeast Asia include countries of all sizes and shapes and with very different ratios of population to natural resources. On the one hand, population presses hard upon available supplies of land in Pakistan, India, Ceylon, and Java. On the other hand, Burma, Thailand, Malaya, Vietnam, and most of Indonesia enjoy highly favorable man-land ratios. Nevertheless, climate, history, and culture have impressed upon the region as a whole characteristics that distinguish it from the rest of the underdeveloped world. Most of this area has been occupied by civilizations that were old when the West was still young. Institutions and attitudes inherited from the past are frequently ill-adapted to the organizational technical requirements of industrialization. In the words of a Western observer, the problem may be not so much "one of economic growth within an existing social framework but the replacement of one civilization by another."[16]

Most of the countries in the region have recently emerged from conditions of colonial conquest, occupation, and administration. The impact of colonialism on current prospects for development is various, but in certain important respects it has created a strong disposition toward a governmentally dominated development process. The close association in the public mind of large-scale private enterprise with colonialism works in that direction. Since, in a number of countries, present governments have come to power invested with the popular enthusiasm that surrounds local heroes who succeed in striking off the foreign tyrants' yoke, there is a natural disposition to look to these leaders for the economic as well as the political benefits of freedom. This disposition, moreover, is strengthened by the fact that inherited social institutions and values are not very conducive to the emergence of economic leaders via the route of private enterprise. Finally, at least in those countries that have enjoyed the benefits of British colonialism, there exists a carefully selected and experienced civil service with strong tradition and high prestige. This civil service, moreover, is not beset by doubts concerning its capacity to undertake the task of economic development. For these reasons and others, I would expect in most of South and Southeast Asia, that, although current wealth and income are predominantly in private hands, governments will play a large role in the attempt to set economic development in motion.

Chapter Two

Government and Business in Nineteenth-Century Economic Development

As we saw in the first chapter, both our experience and received doctrine predispose us to the view that the optimal relationship between government and business in the process of development is one in which government pretty much limits itself to the provision of social and economic overhead and the shaping of an environment favorable to private enterprise. But we are confronted by the fact that, although the existing distribution of economic activity in most undeveloped areas is mainly in private hands, government, in a large part of the underdeveloped world, is looked to as the prime instigator of future economic growth. Moreover, a substantial body of opinion appears to be convinced, for various reasons, that what private enterprise accomplished in the nineteenth century can now only be accomplished by public action. The relation of government to business in the process of economic development differs among regions, mainly because of cultural and historical differences; but almost everywhere the role of government is large.

Let us turn now to what must inevitably be a very broad-brush painting of government-business relationships in the economic development of the West. Our primary concern, in the examination of these relationships, is with their relevance, if any, to the situation confronting countries now seeking the road to economic growth. And it will be found, I think, that this experience is at least as important for an understanding of what is not applicable, and why, as it is for an understanding of what is.

I

A question that confronts us at the outset is—how far back historically, do we need to go in our search for the relevant and irrelevant in the experience of the West? As I pointed out in the first chapter, most underdeveloped countries, by almost any test of economic development, are substantially behind the stage that western Europe—and certainly Britain—had reached in 1800. This might suggest that these countries have a long period of preparation to be undertaken before they are ready for the economic expansion that the nineteenth century brought to the West. On the other hand, the fact that the industrialized parts of the world have already experienced two centuries or more of active development would appear to provide the currently underdeveloped world with extensive opportunities for borrowing. Can these countries, in the words of Lockwood, an historian of Japanese economic development, "simply import the Industrial Revolution from abroad, uncrate it like a piece of machinery, and set it in motion?"[1]

Certain countries, particularly in the Middle East, seem to be attempting something very much like this. Iran and Iraq, in particular, blessed by large oil revenues, are engaged in an extensive importation of Western technology, and a construction, under government auspices, of large-scale development facilities, without preceding or concomitant changes in political and social institutions. It remains to be seen how successful this effort will be.

It has become customary in the literature of economic development to draw a distinction between the pre-conditions of economic growth and the "take-off" into a sustained development process.[2] The "take-off" is usually characterized by a rapid increase in the community's savings ratio, the coming of active industrialization, a significant decline in the death rate and in the percentage of the labor force employed in agriculture, rapid technological change, and the emergence of a sizeable business class enjoying a position of prestige in the community. Once the new savings ratio, the process of technical change, and the development of entrepreneurship have, if I may use the term, become institutionalized, a self-sustained growth process is in motion. The pre-conditions of economic development, on the other hand, though recognized as important, are usually not specified in detail. This is a problem that tends to get swept under the carpet—at least by most economic commentators.

But, if it is true that in parts of the underdeveloped world these pre-conditions have not yet been met, the question of how they are to be met and the relevance of Western experience is a matter of some importance. It is obviously presumptuous, in the time and space available, to attempt to summarize the relevance of at least two centuries of European experience to the industrial revolution that followed; nor, given time and space, have I the competence to do so. Let me, however, mention certain obvious considerations and, for the rest, express the opinion that, for a substantial part of the underdeveloped world, a study of the pre-conditions of growth is at least as important as a study of the characteristics of the growth process itself.

The growth process everywhere in the West took place within the territories of well established nation-states. The period during which, in Heckscher's phrase, "the feudal combination of cosmopolitan universalism and local particularism was giving way to the modern nation-state," was a long one marked in many areas by revolution, violence, and sharp changes in the locus of political power. This same period witnessed the emergence of Western science and, what is more important, the fairly wide diffusion of scientific habits of thought. A new sense of the importance of quantity and of the character of exact methods permeated the environment.[3] Religious revolutions and counter revolutions changed man's conception of his duties and obligations to other men and to society. Geographical discoveries not only opened up new opportunities both for exploration and development, but equally important, opened men's minds to the character of the physical world. In other words, the establishment of the pre-conditions of economic growth in the West involved not only changes in the political environment, but changes in habits of thought, in moral standards, and in human motivations.

That equivalent or similar changes will have to take place in many underdeveloped areas before rapid economic growth is possible goes, I think, without saying. To specify the elements in the culture of these areas that now inhibit growth and will have to be changed if rapid development is to become possible would take us into the, for me, unfamiliar field of comparative anthropology. It may be possible to indicate some of the pertinent considerations by quoting a fellow economist who has had the courage—perhaps rashness is a better word—to penetrate this jungle.

"The stress on quality rather than performance as the basis for personal relationships may or may not have a deterrent effect on interest in the physical world, but at best it provides no positive basis for such interest. The diffuseness of one's obligations to one's family and to community groups requires one to spend one's energies in conventional ways. To divert time and energy to strange activities such as observing nature or tinkering with tools, lessens one's time available for performing the economic, religious, and other ceremonial performances expected of one, and in addition indicates low valuation of these duties. It thus leads to social disapproval. . . ."

And Hagen continues: "Finally, the class structure creates barriers to technological change. Any important economic innovation is apt to alter relative social position."[4]

The central point I am making is that the several centuries preceding industrialization were required in the West to bring about a political structure, habits of thought, and motivations favorable to economic development. These or similar changes presumably constitute the pre-conditions of economic development in a substantial part of the currently underdeveloped world, although there is no good reason to suppose that a similar time period is required to bring them about.

II

To Marx, of course, the changes that we have called the pre-conditions of economic growth were brought about by a particular class pursuing its interests within the context of a particular mode of production. The bourgeoisie, in striking off the shackles of feudalism, shaped at the same time the political and economic institutions and induced and promoted those habits of thought, moral values, and motivations that made possible capitalist economic development. In so deterministic a system the relationship of government to business is simply a function of the stage of development. The question of an optimal relationship can hardly arise since there is no historically possible alternative.

If the pre-conditions of development were the same in currently underdeveloped areas as in early capitalism and if these pre-conditions could be brought about only by the same forces, the history of Western development would, of course, be directly relevant to the present-day problems of economic growth. Under such circumstances, we could look forward presumably to the emergence of business oriented governments seeking to promote economic development by granting maximum freedom of action to private initiative. Whatever Marx may have thought of such possibilities, they are not considered probable by modern Marxists. Since the views of modern Marxists are immediately concerned with the prospective roles of government and business in underdeveloped areas and since certain writers would appear to deny completely the relevance to this question of nineteenth-century experience, it is necessary to say a word or two about these views before returning to our main subject.

Recently two American writers on the problems of economic development have put the issue sharply: Paul Baran, writing "On the Political Economy of Backwardness,"[5] and Martin Bronfenbrenner, writing on "The Appeal of Confiscation in Economic Development."[6] Both implicitly deny the relevance of nineteenth-century experience in, at least, a substantial part of the underdeveloped world. Although the arguments of Baran, who is a good Marxist, differ substantially from those of Bronfenbrenner, who is a strong non-Marxist, they come to much the same conclusion. I suggest that anyone concerned with the prospective relations of government to business in the process of economic development must come to terms with these propositions.

Baran, as a good Marxist, argues that the establishment of the preconditions of economic growth in the West was the work of the middle class; that is, destroying the institutions of feudalism and building up a political structure capable of serving these class interests, within, of course, the determining context of the capitalist mode of production. In the currently underdeveloped areas, however, a sizeable and important business class has had no chance to develop and exert effective political influence before being confronted by socialistic and laboristic demands on the part of the masses. Faced with these demands, the weak business groups have sought the protection of and joined forces with—rather than attempted to destroy—the feudal elements in backward areas. Therefore, Baran concludes: "The possibility of solving the economic and political deadlock prevailing in the underdeveloped countries on lines of progressive capitalism all but disappeared."[7]

In further elaboration of his argument, Baran points out that the influence of the West has not succeeded in raising per capita incomes in much of the underdeveloped world, though it has, by public health measures, enormously increased the size of populations. But without raising per capita incomes it has, nevertheless, through the introduction of cash crops and the development of markets, profoundly disrupted the social cohesion of these old societies. The disruption of family and community relationships in the absence of any alternative leadership, has left the uprooted proletariat an easy prey to socialist and communist ideologies.

Could not, however, asks Baran, "an appropriate policy on the part of the governments involved change the political climate and facilitate economic growth?"[8] His answer, in effect, is that this depends on what interests and what elements in the social structure the government represents. It is unlikely, he thinks, that a government representing the interests of feudal landlords and a nascent, and somewhat rapacious, business group will be able to provide a climate propitious to economic growth along capitalist lines.

Bronfenbrenner's thesis is much less doctrinaire, though it emphasizes some of the same considerations. "The issue we discuss," he says, "is not whether confiscation can be justified by some accepted or conventional occidental standard of morals or propriety, but merely whether it brings the pragmatic results desired, namely, economic development without sacrifice to the scale of living of the mass of the population."

His answer is forthright, to say the least. "It will be our contention that confiscation has done so, is doing so, and will continue to do so, by shifting income to developmental investment from capitalists' consumption, from transfer abroad, and from unproductive investment like luxury housing."

Bronfenbrenner's thesis rests on the presumptions that property incomes, at least in certain underdeveloped areas, are sizeable; that, contrary to early Western experience, these incomes are largely absorbed in luxurious consumption; that, when invested, a substantial part of this investment cannot properly be called developmental; and that the kind of democratic governments that exist in the underdeveloped world, will find it difficult, if not impossible, to divert these incomes to productive use. It cannot be said, particularly in countries where a large percent of property incomes are derived from land holdings in concentrated ownership, that these presumptions are without merit.

Granting the existence of governments sufficiently well organized to invest productively the property incomes now withheld from development, it is easy to devise, as Bronfenbrenner does, a model indicating the effect on per capita incomes of the increased rate of capital formation that confiscation would make possible. And no doubt confiscation, or what will be called confiscation by various groups in the community, will play a role in the development programs of a number of now underdeveloped countries. But it is difficult to accept so economically rational and unpolitical a basis for projecting a course of events in the underdeveloped world. A government capable of carrying out a rational policy of confiscation to promote economic development will, in all probability, be a government that has come to power for other reasons.

Without accepting the extremes of either Baran's Marxian orthodoxy or of Bronfenbrenner's economic rationalism, it is, nevertheless, difficult to avoid at least partial agreement with their diagnosis as applied to certain areas in the underdeveloped world. Existing social relationships, income distributions, individual values, and human motivations are so inhibiting to economic development of any sort; and the existing governments so unwilling to, or incapable of, initiating change, that it is hard to see how the elementary pre-conditions of development can be established short of political revolution. And it seems unlikely, if political revolution does occur, that it will bring to power governments dedicated to the promotion of economic development along nineteenth-century lines.

Having issued the warning, then, that Western experience of economic growth may be irrelevant to certain parts of the underdeveloped world and of limited relevance in others, let us turn to a consideration of some aspects of the relation of government to business in the nineteenth century.

III

The development we are concerned with presupposes the existence of the "pre-conditions" of growth, however these are defined. And this development is roughly coterminous with the process of industrialization. This may be approximately dated in Britain as the last quarter of the eighteenth century, the second quarter of the nineteenth century in France, Germany, and the United States, the fourth quarter in the Scandinavian countries and Japan, and around the turn of the century in Canada and Australia. There is no very great precision in these dates, nor shall I rely on them to support observations of any consequence. They serve merely to remind us that the initiation of economic development, in so far as it is coterminous with active industrialization, covered a period of substantial length and that, presumably, latecomers enjoyed an opportunity of learning something from the experience of those who had gone before.

Some of the broad generalizations that appear to spring from this experience and that may have some relevance to countries now undertaking development programs may be summarized as follows: first, the relations of government to business at similar stages of development cover a very wide spectrum even in countries which can all be called capitalist; second, with development, the role of government inevitably increases for purely technical reasons regardless of changes in ideological views concerning the proper relations of government to business; third, the differences in governmental-business relationships among countries at similar stages in their development are the resultant of many forces both physical and historical.

Among the countries that may be said to have achieved a sustained growth process in the nineteenth century, Britain and Japan stand at opposite poles with respect to the importance of the role assumed by government in the promotion of this process. While it is misleading to say with the economic historian, Knowles, that "A peculiarity of British industrial development in the nineteenth century lay in the fact that it owed practically nothing to state aid,"[9] it is a fact that in the early provision of economic and social overhead capital, Britain stands in a class by itself. Apart from the postal service, the direct contribution of government to the early expansion of transportation and communications system was small.

Eighteenth-century roads in Britain were built and maintained by local parish authorities relying heavily on compulsory labor. But the demand for through communication by wheeled vehicles was largely met by private capital, usually under joint public and private management. The early turnpike trusts were financed by private loans secured by tolls, while management was in the hands of trustees, partly private and partly public. Although turnpike trusts were disappearing from the scene by the 1830's, they had made a large contribution toward the provision of overland transport during the early stages of British industrialization.

The great age of canal building began around 1750 and was from the first almost exclusively handled by private joint-stock companies. Although the improvement of harbors and rivers was under the control of government, the provision of piers and other loading facilities was almost entirely in private hands until late in the nineteenth century. Needless to say, shipping was entirely a field for private enterprise.

All the English railways were constructed by private enterprise, each under a particular act of Parliament. The only aid given by the state was, in Clapham's words, "that really great interference with property, the right to buy land compulsorily."[10] Although maximum railway rates were established by public authority from the beginning, they were almost invariably too high to be operative. The only serious regulation attempted by government was concerned with safety measures, and even these were relatively ineffective until late in the century.

The early provision of urban facilities in Britain was also undertaken by private enterprise. Gas and water works were predominantly built and run by private interests, although dividend limitations were imposed by public authority. When electric lighting became feasible later in the century, Parliament gave priority to municipal undertakings, but most of the field was initially occupied by private companies. Even in education, the most important of the social overhead undertakings in relation to development, government did surprisingly little during the early period of industrialization. Thus as late as 1858, only 25 percent of school financing was undertaken by the state; the remainder came from fees and private subscriptions.[11]

The primary explanation of the limited role played by government in the provision of social and economic overhead capital in Britain is not, I think, ideological. As I suggested in the first chapter, Adam Smith envisaged as an important function of the state the construction and maintenance of those public works and institutions that private individuals had no interest in providing. This, in general, was the position of the so-called laissez-faire economists in Britain. Even Bentham, commonly regarded— though probably mistakenly—as one of the most extreme exponents of the philosophy of natural liberty did not quarrel with this view.[12] Furthermore, in areas in which private enterprise lagged in the provision of overhead facilities, government did, as a matter of fact, intervene. The real question is why private enterprise was so much more able and willing to undertake these tasks in Britain than in other countries.

A large part of the answer, I feel sure, is that Britain, on the eve of industrialization, was substantially more developed economically than most other countries at this stage. Not only did the provision of overhead facilities represent favorable opportunities for private investment, but private funds were available for investment. In Britain the construction of turnpikes, canals, and railways was not in anticipation of traffic that might develop over the next few decades. The potential traffic was at hand. By 1800, per capita incomes and the rate of savings in Britain were already relatively high. Furthermore, the financial institutions required to channel these savings into productive investment were available. However, there is one particular source of savings, peculiar to Britain, at least in degree, and for which the state had a special responsibility; it deserves mention.

The acquisition of overseas territories during the seventeenth and eighteenth centuries offered Britain market opportunities and cheap sources of supply that undoubtedly had a significant effect on the rate of profits. Anti-colonial writers and Marxian economists see in the "Rape of Bengal" and in the other imperialistic activities the principal source of financing for the industrial revolution. While this is certainly not true, it is probably correct that the accumulation of private profit from overseas ventures is one of the reasons why capital was so easily available in Britain for investment in overhead facilities. In this indirect way, the state may be said to have intervened in the promotion of economic development. A more important type of intervention, however, lay in the development of a legal and administrative framework within which private enterprise could flourish.

*   *   *

Japan's industrialization may be said to have been actively initiated after the Meiji Restoration in 1868. The role of the government in the provision of capital, the allocation, and the management of resources was a dominant one in early Japanese economic development. Savings appear to have attained a high ratio to national income very early in the development process. In part, this came about because of the extreme inequality of income distribution, coupled with the relatively low consumption expenditures of large income receivers. But voluntary savings were heavily supplemented by government savings from the yields, principally, of land and other agricultural taxes. The Japanese government seems to have been one of the few governments, outside the Communist world, capable of effective taxation of agricultural income.

Not only did the Japanese government play an active role in expanding resource availability, but it exercised extensive control over the direction of investment. According to one expert, G. C. Allen, "It can be said with truth that there was scarcely an important Japanese industry of the Western type during the later decades of the nineteenth century which did not owe its establishment to state initiative."[13] The state directed investment by establishing publicly owned enterprises, by undertaking joint ventures with private capital, by subsidizing private investment and guaranteeing returns, as well as through its extensive purchasing operations for military and civilian account. In the decade after 1868 the state, entirely apart from the provision of overhead facilities, built and operated such diverse enterprises as coal, copper, and gold mines; iron foundries; shipyards;

machine shops; model factories in cement, paper, glass, sulphuric acid, cotton spinning, and many others.[14] Needless to say, the overhead facilities that in Britain were so largely undertaken by private enterprise, were, in Japan, constructed by government.

A recitation, however, of the activities of government in the promotion of economic development is apt to lead to an undervaluation of the contribution of private enterprise to the economic growth of Japan. Government ventures in many industries were in the nature of demonstration models, and the bulk of the development in these industries was, in fact, in private hands. Moreover, most of the government's industrial enterprises were transferred to private investors after 1882. Small-scale industry, which appears to have been more important in Japan than in most other countries at a similar stage of development, has been entirely a private affair. If government exercised an important role in the direction of investment early in the development process, later industrial expansion and the choice of production methods were almost entirely private. Doubtless this accounts for the fact that the very extensive technological borrowing from abroad has been carefully adapted to the factor proportions existing in Japan.[15] Japanese technological processes have always been labor intensive and have adjusted slowly to the increasing availability of capital. The mistakes common to so many underdeveloped countries of importing the newest in technology regardless of the scarcity of capital and the plentitude of labor seems to have been largely avoided.

Undoubtedly the government's most important contribution in the area of social overhead was the attention paid in Japan to education. The Japanese government, moreover, seems to have adapted its educational expenditures more specifically to development purposes than has been customary in the Western world. Individuals and groups were dispatched in large numbers to study Western science, administration, and techniques. Western experts were brought to Japan to provide technical assistance to all of Japan's developing industries. In addition to establishing a system of compulsory primary education throughout the country, the government created technical schools in large numbers.

Under this forced draft development, the national income of Japan increased at a more rapid rate than that of any other country in the nineteenth century.[16] The view is frequently expressed in Asia that this growth rate is no more than could be expected with independence and that had the countries of Southern Asia not been hamstrung by colonial control, they too might have experienced a similar rate of development. Certainly independence was a necessary condition, but as some of the countries of Southern Asia are now discovering, it is not sufficient.

The extremely high rate of capital formation in Japan was to a considerable extent, as I have indicated above, dependent on a highly skewed distribution of income. Government policy, so far as it had a significant effect, tended to intensify this situation through the characteristics of the tax structure and the types of assistance granted to private investors. In the absence of developed securities markets, the high percent of savings from large incomes that was customary in Japan tended to be invested directly or deposited in banks lending at long, as well as short, term.[17] Furthermore, although per capita incomes rose rapidly, wage rates and working class standards of living lagged behind—at least during the first few decades of development. According to one observer, "The mass toleration of the economic squeeze may be traced ultimately to population pressure, lack of organization, traditional docility, and patriotic fervor."[18] It is to be doubted whether these sources of capital formation can be as effectively tapped by countries now attempting to accelerate the process of development, at least in Southern Asia.

A substantial part of the success of the Japanese government's active intervention in the field of industry is to be attributed to the fact that it came on the scene at a late stage. This observation is even more applicable to industrialization in Communist countries. A review of the circumstances under which the early stages of industrialization took place in Britain and elsewhere leads one to doubt whether this process could have been accomplished in any economy directed or extensively controlled by government. The early developments in industrial technology were undertaken not by men of science who discovered the practical application of general principles but by skilled artisans and tinkerers working in the eighteenth-century equivalent of the twentieth-century garage. The exploitation of new techniques was in the hands of individual and family firms operating in an environment relatively free from government control. Profits were high and losses frequent in this era of Schumpeterian entrepreneurship.[19] It is difficult, if not inconceivable, to believe, that government agencies could have accomplished or significantly furthered this task.

To the extent that technical innovation still depends on this kind of economic and intellectual freedom and this type of business organization, the case against a serious measure of government intervention is, on purely developmental grounds, strong. Once these techniques have been developed, however, they can be borrowed. And if their modern application requires large-scale units whose operation lies outside the capabilities of the family-sized firm, borrowing by government as well as by private agencies may be feasible. Furthermore, insofar as subsequent technical change is more a matter of laboratory investigation than of individual tinkering, this possibility is strengthened. I shall return to these considerations in the next chapter. Here it is sufficient to note that at an advanced stage of industrialization, large-scale intervention by the Japanese government *was* highly successful in accomplishing a transfer of the technical and administrative experience of the West.

Finally, it seems highly unlikely that the forced draft industrialization undertaken in Japan *could* have been carried through without extensive government participation. Not only did the advanced stage of development elsewhere make this participation possible, but without this participation it is probable that the rate of economic growth in Japan would have been much slower. A strong government enjoying popular support has opportunities for marshalling and organizing human efforts and enlisting popular support for any goal, including economic development, that private enterprise, by its very nature, cannot enjoy. The Japanese development took place in a very special environment in which the country's precarious security position released a strong patriotic fervor for development as a necessary condition of continued independence. But the Japanese example of government induced economic growth has not been lost on governments of other Asian countries now seeking development.

Governmental-business relationships in other countries experiencing growth in the nineteenth century lie somewhere between the British and Japanese extremes. In none of these countries was the role of business as large as in the early stages of British development; in none was the part played by government as significant as in Japan. It is impossible to say more here concerning this range of experience, but I cannot leave the subject of governmental-business relationships in the nineteenth century without referring briefly to this relationship in the economic growth of the United States.

IV

The remarks I have to make on the American experience fall under four main considerations:

1. It is clear by now that government played a much larger role in early American economic development than was commonly supposed until fairly recently or than is commonly assumed in business circles today.

2. Adhering to our tripartite distinction of government participation in

the expansion, allocation, and management of resource use, it may be said, however, that public action to promote development in the United States was directed much more to expansion than to allocation and management.

3. Moreover, in contrast to the roles now played by governments in many underdeveloped areas, and assumed by government in the early development of Japan, I have the impression that the initiative for public action in the United States came to a much greater extent from private business interests and local groups than from attempts to apply any very carefully matured public policy.

4. For this reason and for others, although it may be said that the central government, or at least parts of the government, have had, at times, a national development policy, it has never been a very consistent or persistent policy, and few steps were ever taken to develop the governmental machinery necessary to put a consistent policy into effect.

During the last decade or two, extensive research on the economic activities of the federal, state, and local governments has indicated that government played a much larger part in early nineteenth-century development than our strong tradition of free enterprise would lead one to expect. Surveying the literature on internal improvements, Carter Goodrich observes, "Recent studies . . . have shown that the volume of government investment was greater than had been believed, both in absolute figures and in relation to total canal and railroad investment, to total national investment, and to the total budgets of governmental authorities. Yet, half a century ago, the first modern student of the subject, Guy Stevens Callender, was able to point out that our supposedly individualistic America had had in the early and middle nineteenth century a certain world prominence as an example of the extension of the state into industry."[20]

Certainly as compared to Britain, the activity of American governments in the provision of economic overhead capital was impressive. Whereas British canals were constructed entirely on private initiative, the American canal system was built by government enterprise or as a mixed public and private undertaking. The early railways also were mainly joint enterprises with state and local governments contributing heavily to capital requirements. Even in the case of predominantly private ventures, the federal government undertook the surveying of canal, turnpike, and railway rights of way and frequently offered engineering assistence in construction. Fourteen army engineers, for example, were engaged betwen 1827–30 on the survey and construction of the Baltimore and Ohio Railway. This enterprise, in the words of one authority, "served as a valuable training school for railway engineering as the construction of the Erie Canal had for canal engineering." [21] Hill also notes that "From 1816 onward the Army Engineers (established in 1802) made exploratory surveys of western rivers and lakes and gave engineering aid and advice to state and local navigation projects along the Atlantic coast." [22]

The principal governmental assistance to public works in the first half of the nineteenth century, however, came from state and local governments. The first federal land grants to railways date from 1850. Before then the principal form of federal assistance, apart from engineering aid previously mentioned, was tariff remission on the import of necessary materials. State and local governments, on the other hand, were important contributors to the capital requirements of early turnpike, canal, and railway construction. The Pennsylvania Railway was largely constructed, in Pennsylvania, from the stock purchases of the municipalities through which it passed. The state of Pennsylvania participated as owner in some hundred and fifty mixed corporations. As Louis Hartz, the historian of public economic activity in this state has noted, the early period of development was definitely not dominated by laissez-faire. "Far from being limited, the objectives of the state in the economic field were usually so broad that they were beyond its administrative powers to achieve." [23]

It may be fairly said, however, that the principal developmental objectives of both federal and local governments lay rather in the expansion than in the allocation of resource use. To be sure, the tariff policy of the federal government gave a powerful impetus to industrialization, but this policy was not selective in any discernible economic sense. Apart from tariff policy, the principal activities of the federal government in the promotion of development lay in assistance to transportation—particularly after 1850—and in its land policy. Both of these were primarily frontier phenomena, and the main objective was to secure as rapid as possible an expansion, through settlement, of resource use. Strongly reinforcing this objective, as Fowke has emphasized, was the fear that a failure to settle the land to the west would encourage the encroachment of foreign powers. [24] Concerning the activities of state and local governments in the field of public works, their primary interests lay in expansion, and frequently competitive expansion as against other states and areas. Both federal and local governments were quite content to leave to private enterprise and the free market the direction of development.

Nor was government in the United States much interested in management. The primary aim of public assistance was to accelerate the expansion of private enterprise. Even those ventures to which government capital contributions were large were mainly run by private interests. As Hartz suggests, "What was needed, given the great scope of economic policy, was a stable and expert administration. It did not develop."[25] This is true not only of the state but of the federal government, and there are reasons for this failure. Perhaps the chief one was the existence of a broad consensus of opinion favoring the free market and private management. While western European countries saw a gradual development of an ideology favoring government intervention in economic affairs, the trend in the United States was rather in the opposite direction. This country was more strongly laissez-faire in the decades after 1860 than it ever had been in the first half of the century. This trend suggests that the significant role of government in the promotion of early American development was not so much a matter of desire as of necessity.

A consideration of the pressures that led to government action tends to reinforce this view. In marked contrast to the current situation in most underdeveloped countries, state and local governments—and sometimes the federal government also—were forced into action by the demands of their constituency who frequently found the provision of economic overhead facilities outside the realm of private competence. The provision of these facilities was not something that was planned from the center. Rather it was demanded by and frequently financed by localities. When private capital was lacking and state action was constitutionally forbidden, the citizens of Cincinnati proceeded to organize and construct the Cincinnati Southern as a municipal venture. In noting this and other examples, Carter Goodrich is led to observe that:

"The building of the American network of transportation gained support from the local patriotism and the booster spirit of the city, town, and small community. It may be pointed out that the Communist practice of carrying regimentation and the party apparatus down into the smallest units, and the very different methods of "community development" of India and other countries, represent deliberate efforts to obtain popular participation at the local level in the processes of economic development. In the United States, vigorous local participation took instead the spontaneous forms that have been described."[26]

The importance of local initiative and regional interests and the concentration of governmental action on the expansion rather than on the direction or management of resource use have a bearing on the question whether, and in what sense, the economic growth of the United States may be said to have been shaped by a conscious development policy. Certainly there was a persistent consensus of political opinion on the need for the acquisition and rapid settlement of the hinterland stretching to the Pacific. The federal public lands policy and assistance to western railways was an expression of that consensus. It must be remembered, however, that security considerations were as much involved here as any deliberate intention to promote economic growth. Certainly also tariff policy played an important part in shaping early American economic development. In a sense, this policy may be said to have expressed an underlying strategy of development best expressed in Hamilton's Report on Manufactures. But when one considers the impact on U. S. tariff policy of private and regional interests, one is forced to the conclusion that the emerging policy probably was more in the nature of a compromise among local interests than an expression of a well-considered development strategy.

It must be remembered that in the early stages of economic development, state and local governments played a much more active role than central authority. State activity was motivated by considerations of regional competition to a degree that casts doubt on the dominant influence of any general strategy of development even if it can be said that the federal government possessed one. Furthermore, the failure at both the state and federal level to develop a public service capable of administering a strong development policy is a relevant consideration.

The policy of leaving economic development to private initiative and local interests is, of course, nonetheless a development policy. Furthermore, under democratic government, as we shall see later, even the most centralized phases of development, to a considerable extent, are inevitably shaped by local interests. The distinction, then, between a development policy that assigns to government the primary role of initiating and maintaining conditions propitious to the functioning of private enterprise and the free market, and a development policy that assigns to government a positive role in the implementation of a conscious strategy of development, is only one of degree. As I read American history, our development policy, to the extent we may be said to have had one, was much closer to the former than to the latter. The fact that governments in the United States undertook a much more active role in the provision of social and economic overhead facilities than did government in Britain was much more the resultant of a difference in economic situation than a difference in ideology. Economic growth in the United States was at no stage shaped by a deliberate and positive development policy in the sense that Japanese growth may be said to have been shaped.

V

In summary, what can be said about the relevance of nineteenth-century economic growth to the situation of underdeveloped countries now seeking development? In certain parts of the underdeveloped world it needs to be stressed that the pre-conditions of growth have not yet been met. In these areas the availability of financial resources either from domestic or foreign sources may permit the construction of impressive facilities and the transplantation of Western techniques; but without deeper political and social changes, the initiation of a sustained growth process is dubious. An acute observer of the development process has drawn a distinction between planting the seeds and transplanting the fruits of development. "The awkward fact is that it is very much easier to transplant the fruits of economic development, than to transplant the seeds." As an example, Singer points out that it is fatally easy to "set up an elaborate machinery of state planning, and under the conditions obtaining in many underdeveloped areas such machinery often becomes absurdly irrelevant to real needs and possibilities."[27]

The establishment of the pre-conditions of economic growth is so handicapped by existing political interests in some underdeveloped areas as to make it unlikely that much can be accomplished without a forceable overthrow of those interests. The revolutionary movement need not be Communist, though I do not have much doubt that in certain countries it may be. Needless to say, in those countries the nineteenth-century experience will have little relevance to subsequent development. In some other countries the establishment of the pre-conditions is apt to be a slow process marked by much social unrest and political instability, though not necessarily tending in a Communist direction.

Latin America would appear to be the region most likely to develop somewhat along the lines of Western economic growth. Most countries in Latin America have a sizeable business community continually replenished by migration from western Europe. Foreign private capital and technology are, moreover, available in sizeable quantities, and local business participation is increasingly sought. Even in Latin America, however, the role of government in promoting development is apt to be larger than in any of the advanced Western countries at a similar stage of their development.

In those Asian countries that are ripe for economic growth, governmental-business relationships are more apt to resemble the Japanese relationships in an early stage of development than those characteristic of Western economic growth. Indigenous business groups are small in most Asian countries, and the opportunities for foreign private investment are nowhere near as great as in Latin America. In a number of these countries, moveover, a governmental structure and a public service which have been inherited from the colonial period are much better equipped to play an active role in the development process than were many Western governments at a similar stage of their country's development. These Asian governments are imbued with a determination to initiate economic growth similar to that which motivated the Japanese government and envisage a strong and positive economic development program as the only way of accomplishing this end.

The role for private enterprise and for foreign private investment in many parts of the underdeveloped world will continue to be large, but in no area is it likely that the environment will be permeated with the laissez-faire philosophy characteristic of early nineteenth-century growth. One of the important reasons is that nowhere in the underdeveloped world does there exist a population as prepared for economic development and industrialization as were the early nineteenth-century populations of the West. Even if there were, however, it is the contention of an important school of thought that economic development in the present age demands a much larger role for government than has been traditional in the West. The next chapter will examine this contention.

Chapter Three

Government Initiated Development

In the first chapter we were concerned with the contrast between traditional notions of the proper role of government in the process of development and the role as commonly conceived in most underdeveloped countries. The second chapter considered the relevance and irrelevance of nineteenth-century experience to the situation now confronting these countries. As we have seen, there are those who would deny the relevance of nineteenth-century experience, at least for a large part of the underdeveloped world, on the Marxian ground that the political forces that paved the way for capitalist development are inadequate to undertake that task today. To another group of students of the development process, the nineteenth-century experience seems largely irrelevant on grounds that are mainly economic. Although earlier economic development was primarily the work of individual initiative, significant differences in the present situation appear to call for extensive government action.

The principal lines of argument in support of this view were suggested in the first chapter under the headings, the case for government initiated expansion; the case for public direction of investment; and the case for public management. Here I propose to return to these considerations for more detailed examination. Although for purposes of analysis I separate these lines of argument, it is evident that, in certain respects, they are mutually reinforcing. The case for a simultaneous expansion of investment in a number of directions rests in part on the proposition that these are economies of scale, including external economies, that cannot be effectively realized by a piecemeal investment process. But simultaneous expansion of a type necessary to maximize these advantages presupposes a considerable direction of investment; that is, of planning. Furthermore, government initiation of investment and planning may provide an environment congenial to public management and vice versa. Despite the interconnections, it will be useful, for purposes of analysis, to separate these propositions. I propose to introduce this discussion with some general remarks on the subject of planning.

I

There are two central notions in the concept of planning that need to be separated for further scrutiny. One is the notion of action based on a careful assessment of the future. "Behavior governed by conscious expectations," declares Boulding, "is what we mean by 'planning' . . ."[1] The second notion is suggested in Polanyi's distinction between "deliberate order" and "spontaneous order." Deliberate order "consists in limiting the freedom of things and men to stay or move about at their pleasure, by assigning to each a specific position in a prearranged plan." Spontaneous order, on the other hand, refers to an "equilibrium achieved by the mutual interaction of particles or individuals in a system."[2]

Both ideas are necessary to the concept of planning. If we leave out the notion of control, planning becomes equivalent to any deliberate act of choice. Any unit, including the individual personality, becomes a planning unit; and any governmental policy, no matter how libertarian, is planning. This appears to approach Hayek's conception of a "plan" as the sum total of economic activity. The fundamental question, he says, is who does the planning. This also appears to be the view of those who equate government planning with public economic policy. Planning to them is a process, "neutral" towards authority and freedom, centralization and decentralization; and any exercise of forethought becomes a "plan." Anyone is free to use words as he sees fit, and admittedly, this is one possible meaning of planning. According to this usage, all economies are planned economies since, in even the most libertarian economy, individual action takes place within some set of common rules.

There is another concept of planning that puts the whole emphasis on control. According to this concept, planning requires that all economic activities be subject to a central determination. In a planned economy there is no room for individual economic initiative, for buying or selling, for markets or for money. This is essentially the Von Mises conception of socialist planning, and it is on the basis of this definition that he has little difficulty in demonstrating that a socialist state cannot act rationally.[3] Polanyi advances a similar notion of planning as "direct physical controls, consciously applied from the centre" without benefit of markets or the use of money.[4] Consequently, he concludes, in even stronger terms than Mises, that central planning is "impossible in the same sense in which it is impossible for a cat to swim the Atlantic."[5] Complete centralization of authority brings about a situation in which the information required for rational choice lies outside the competence of the organization.

Thus we have at one extreme, a definition of planning that would make all economies planned economies and, at the other, one that says planning based on rational calculation is impossible. One conception puts the whole emphasis on the analysis of expectations, the other on the centralization of authority. If, however, we want to understand why, say the Soviet Union, is more of a planned economy than, say the United States, we need to take both considerations into account. If both "control" and "deliberate action" are characteristic of planning, the planning unit must consist of more than one person. It needs to be an organization of individuals, each of whose activities is, in some sense, limited and directed in the interest of the organization. Planning is an organization problem and the organization can be either a sub-unit in an economic system or the system itself.

Whatever the organization and whatever its purposes, a central issue is concerned with the extent to which the process of decision-making should be decentralized. The model of laissez-faire capitalism is an example of extreme decentralization with market prices acting as the principal co-ordinating agency. Even so, markets cannot function competitively without rules laid down by public authority. This extreme of decentralization is inevitably plagued by price and output behavior that diverge from "ideal" behavior even under equilibrium conditions, and these divergences have long been the special study of welfare economics. There is reason to believe, moreover, that in relation to the objectives of economic growth, extreme decentralization of decision-making will produce even greater divergences. There is then a *prima facie* case for moving in the direction of a greater degree of central control over the process of decision-making; and this essentially is the case for planning. Planning inevitably involves an attack on the central importance of the market as a co-ordinating agency; and inevitably, it also involves some substitution of centralized decision-making for the unregulated private reactions to changes in market prices. This does not mean that planning can dispense with the market, and no planned economy, including that of the Soviet Union, attempts to do so. But it does mean that an attempt is made by government to supplement and correct market results by public operations and the control of private activities.

Planning, so defined, is obviously a matter of degree. There are no completely planned and no completely unplanned economies. However, the greater the centralization of decision-making within an organization, the more important the role of planning and, incidentally, the greater the difficulty of assembling and analyzing the data upon which rational decision-making depends. There are difficulties as well as advantages in centralization. [6]

When one examines the comprehensive plans that have been promulgated in many underdeveloped countries, one cannot help being impressed by the extent to which they propose to move in the direction of a "deliberately ordered" rather than a "spontaneously ordered" development. This is not to say that no attention is paid to policies and devices for freeing markets and stimulating individual initiative. On the contrary, in certain plans—Puerto Rico provides the most striking example—planning is strongly oriented in this direction. But, particularly in Southern Asia, development plans in general evince little confidence in the capacity of private initiative and the free market to do the job. These plans are concerned with ways and means of expanding the supply of resources, with the direction of resource use, and with the scope of public and private management. In all three areas the emphasis is on positive public action rather than on the devising of policies that might make private action more effective. In this sense they appear to aim strongly toward a planned development even though, in their present underdeveloped state, these economies could hardly be called planned.

Some of the principal problems of planning revolve around the relation of futurity to the span and character of administrative control. The individual enterprise operating on the free market presumably determines its action largely from signals given to it by changing prices and quantities in the relevant markets and by expectations of future changes that are mainly based on past experience. Both the lateral scope and the time horizon of this information-gathering, decision-making process, say the planners, are too narrow to induce action needed for economic development. External economics are ignored, the possible repercussions of future factor supplies are neglected, the reliance on past experience, which is of stagnation, leads to a faulty estimate of the risks of expansion. On the other hand, the planner, in attempting to take these neglected variables into account, not only faces some formidable problems of data collection and analysis, but must consider the administrative problems connected with putting this new and more perfect calculus into effect. Contemporary planning does not dispense with the market, and makes no pretense to do so, but if the decisions generated by and reflected in changes in the market are to be corrected to take account of development possibilities, this requires either a fairly elaborate system of controls, or a large expansion of the area of public management—or both.

We shall be concerned with some of the administrative aspects of planning in the next chapter. Let me here, however, emphasize one other characteristic of, at least, democratic planning. Any attempt to allocate resources in order to attain development objectives operates in an environment in which there are strong local and group interests with objectives of their own that may or may not fit into a sensible development plan. "The real limitations to planning in a democratic society," according to C. A. R. Crosland, a former Labour Party M. P., "lie not so much in lack of statistical information, appropriate techniques, or administration as in the obstacles presented by political interests."[7] Since a representation of divergent interests is of the essence of democracy, continuous pressure to shape the plan in accordance with such interests must be considered to be an inescapable aspect of democratic planning. The problems then of information gathering and analysis, of administration, and of political pressures, must be kept in mind in assessing the merits of the planning attack on the free market.

II

The case for government initiated expansion rests in part on the thesis that the translation of underdeveloped economies into economies exhibiting a process of sustained growth will require "a big push" or a "critical minimum effort." In part it rests in the sources of funds that are likely to be available to support this effort.

"There is a minimum level of resources that must be devoted to . . . a development program if it is to have any chance of success. Launching a country into self-sustained growth is a little like getting an airplane off the ground. There is a critical ground speed which must be passed before the craft can become air-borne."[8] Supplementing this statement by Milliken and Rostow, another commentator observed, "Proceeding 'bit by bit' will not add up in its effects to the sum total of the single bits. A minimum quantum of investment is a necessary (though not sufficient) condition of success. This is in a nutshell the contention of the theory of the big push."[9]

Quoting another exponent of this thesis, "In order to achieve sustained secular growth . . . it is necessary that the initial stimulant or stimulants to development be of a certain critical minimum size." And, Leibenstein adds, "These stimulants . . . tend to raise per capita incomes above the equilibrium level. But in backward economies, long-run economic development does not occur because the magnitude of the stimulants is too small. That is to say, the efforts to escape from economic backwardness, be they spontaneous or forced, are below the critical minimum required for persistent growth."[10]

Many underdeveloped areas, it is asserted, are currently in a vicious circle in which poverty generates a low rate of savings and investments, and this low level, in turn, sustains an expansion of production facilities no greater than required by relatively low rates of population growth. Any small improvement in productivity, whether brought about by increased investment, technological change, or the opening up of new areas, is likely to generate a population increase that will not only prevent any sustained improvement in living standards but will leave the vicious circle intact. If a sharp rise in the rate of population growth, brought about by the effect on death rates of public health measures, precedes any substantial improvement in productivity, the problem only becomes more difficult.

Insofar as this picture describes the condition in underdeveloped areas —and it must be admitted that it approximates reality in some—it is clear that the achievement of a sustained growth process will require a very substantial increase in productivity. The issues that principally concern us are whether this increase must necessarily take place in large discontinuous steps, rather than via a multitude of small incremental improvements, and whether extensive public action is required to bring it about. These issues are clearly, to some considerable extent, linked.

The currently advanced Western countries managed to handle the population problem created by a rapidly declining death rate, while still achieving a continuous advance in per capita productivity; though it must be emphasized that the problem was nowhere as serious at it now appears to be in the densely populated areas of Southern Asia. As Hagen points out, twenty or more countries during the nineteenth and twentieth centuries escaped this "Malthusian trap."[11] Moreover, most of them did so without any very extensive governmental intervention.

It is maintained, however, that even nineteenth-century growth was not a slow, continuous process but rather that a century or more of persistent evolution was followed by a rapid leap into a situation of sustained and fairly rapid growth. During this relatively short period—two or three decades—of the "take-off" into economic growth, there occurred a rapid rise in the rate of capital formation, quasi-revolutionary improvements in technology, and the emergence of a class of strongly motivated and competent business leaders. These changes were mutually reinforcing and together produced a sharp increase in productivity and per capita incomes.[12]

Statistical information on national incomes and rates of saving, and measures of technical change and of changes in the composition of the labor force are, for the period in question, probably insufficient for the effective testing of this hypothesis. However, we do know enough about differences in growth rates in different countries to raise a doubt concerning the inevitability of a short period take-off in the economic development of all countries. Nevertheless the word "revolution" in the phrase "industrial revolution" does mean something, and it is not necessary to suppose that Western economic growth described the path of a smooth and continuous curve. Without accepting the inevitability of a short period "take-off," it may be said that, insofar as Western economic development was marked by a sharp increase in the rate of capital formation with accompanying technological changes, it tends to support the thesis of the big push.

If the translation of Western economies to a status of sustained growth required a large and discontinuous effort, there are reasons for believing that a similar translation in underdeveloped countries will require an even larger and more discontinuous effort. Some of these reasons are technological, others are psychological and have to do with expectations either spontaneously generated or fed by governments. These considerations are additional to any influence in this direction that may arise out of the fact that most currently underdeveloped countries are, in many respects, at a lower stage of development than Western countries had attained early in the nineteenth century.

The principal technological reasons for thinking that a take-off into sustained growth might require larger capital investment than was experienced under earlier conditions have to do with the fact that presently underdeveloped areas are latecomers. The fact that efficient techniques exist to be borrowed and do not have to be slowly developed at great effort and cost might be thought to be one of the great advantages possessed by countries currently seeking development and, on balance, it certainly is. If this technological heritage were not available, economic growth in the underdeveloped world would undoubtedly be even slower than, under present prospects, it promises to be.

But the technology of the West is capital-intensive, it comes in large units, and it is expensive both in local currency and in foreign exchange.[13] And since the general direction of Western technological development may well have been toward increasing capital intensity, the investment required per additional unit of output is, in some meaningful sense, probably higher than that experienced in earlier development. The more discontinuous, the "lumpier," the investment, the more important the external economies that can only be captured by additional investment. If expansion took place by small increments, it would be conceivable that investment could be so distributed as to make possible continuous and effective use of all increments. A railway, however, has to be installed *en bloc*, and its effective use depends on adequate traffic requirements from other economic activities. A power plant of efficient size will be fully used only if complementary facilities are also installed. It has long been recognized that the growth of the economy as a whole brings with it economies of scale as real as those associated with larger plants and firms. Allyn Young, in a paper that has become classic, considered those economies external to the plant and firm but internal to the community to be one of the principal sources of economic growth.[14] The smaller the incremental investment requirements of the possible areas of expansion, the larger the possibility that these community economies of scale may be realized through a slow and relatively continuous process of capital formation. The larger and more discontinuous the particular investment requirements, the greater the difficulty of realizing these economies without a massive investment program.

These then are the principal technological reasons behind the thesis of the big push. The psychological case stands on quite a different footing. It is, in a sense, irrational but, for all that, in certain parts of the underdeveloped world, important. The fact that the gap between per capita incomes in economically advanced and economically backward countries has been widening rather than narrowing has not escaped the notice of the governments or the literate citizenry of the latter countries. Nor has the extremely rapid growth rate achieved by Soviet Russia and, perhaps, about to be achieved by China. The official Soviet figures tend to be accepted in Southern Asia at face value, but even as scaled down by Western experts, these figures are impressive. The Soviet Union and China are obviously following a Communist version of the big push, and it seems to be paying off. On the one hand, with this demonstration that it can be done and, on the other, the obvious necessity of a rapid rise in national income if the gap separating the underdeveloped world is not to be widened, and indeed, at least partially closed, the pressure for rapid development is understandable.

Furthermore, the pressure is strong for a particular kind of development, one whose achievement would expand enormously the initial capital requirements. It has been said that the myth of the American development ideology is the community development program, while the Soviet myth is the steel mill. There is little doubt which myth is more highly esteemed in most of the underdeveloped world.

It can be seen then that the capital requirements, if a "leap" into sustained economic growth is to be attempted, are very large, and they become even larger if the leap is to the height and in the direction toward which many underdeveloped countries are now aiming. When one looks at these requirements and at the possible sources of funds to satisfy them, it becomes clear that, given the per capita incomes, the income flows, and the state of the capital market in most underdeveloped areas, private investment will not do the trick. It is only a little less clear that public investment will not do it either, but in a number of countries the attempt will be made. In other words, the impact of technology on the capital requirements of early development, the public pressure for haste, the ideological predispositions regarding the character of development, the primitive state of domestic capital markets, and the nature of foreign sources of funds— all stack the cards in favor of government as the primary initiator of resource expansion.

The principal sources of funds for development are, of course, private voluntary savings, compulsory savings generated by inflation, governmental fiscal surpluses, private foreign investment, and foreign governmental and quasi-governmental loans and grants. In a number of underdeveloped countries non-monetary investment plays a considerable role in capital formation, principally in agriculture. Here we are concerned primarily with monetary investment and why these funds tend to flow so largely into public hands. In many underdeveloped countries the principal outlet for savings, apart from direct investment, is in government securities. Such capital markets as exist are strongly oriented towards public rather than private investment. The market for private securities is developing and will develop further. Sensible public policy, moreover, could greatly accelerate that growth. But this kind of development takes time. Meanwhile the differential advantages enjoyed by government as a borrower syphon off a substantial share of private savings for public investment. Public credit could, of course, be made the basis of loans to private enterprise, and in some underdeveloped areas—the Philippines, for example—it is. But this is not what happens typically.

The inflation that frequently accompanied, and sometimes accelerated, nineteenth-century development was largely a product of business borrowing to take advantage of expanding economic opportunities. This source of credit expansion is not unknown in current experience, but increasingly the impulse to rising prices comes from public development programs. In listing the financial resources available for the Second Five Year Plan, the Indian Planning Commission included twelve billion rupees of Central Bank lending which was intended to cover 25 percent of the public sector program. Whereas in the nineteenth century, inflation was regarded as a phenomenon to be avoided, even though frequently it was not avoided, currently, almost everywhere in the underdeveloped world, inflation is considered as an inevitable concomitant and effective stimulant to economic growth. It may well be; I do not argue the contrary. I merely point out that in countries where a large volume of deficit financing is considered a necessary part of an effective development program any resulting compulsory savings are apt to be channeled into government for developmental or other purposes.

The enlargement of government surpluses through changes in the rates and structure of taxes is almost universally thought to be essential to the "big push." Indeed, it is difficult to see how a sharp rise in the savings ratio can be brought about in many underdeveloped countries without creating a large budgetary surplus. The chief question is whether this task lies within the capacity of democratic governments. Recently both India and Pakistan have been making serious attempts to increase tax yields, and certainly this is one important potential route to a higher rate of capital formation. Needless to say, this route lies exclusively in the hands of government.

Until recently foreign private investment has been by far the principal carrier of advanced technology, and in a number of countries it has constituted a significant fraction of total investment. This is still true in the oil countries, and it has been true in important areas of the British Commonwealth. Foreign private direct investment, however, has always been highly selective both as to area and to type of employment. In the currently underdeveloped world, a large section of Latin America, certain parts of Africa south of the Sahara, and the Middle East are the preferred regions. Private foreign investment in Southern Asia currently runs at very small figures, and there is no reason to believe, barring the discovery of oil, that these figures will very greatly increase. Furthermore, even in those countries to which foreign private investment is mainly directed, it accounts, except in oil rich areas, for a small fraction of total investment.

Direct investment abroad, moreover, has moved mainly into the extraction and production of raw materials for export. Although in recent years American investment in manufacturing enterprises has been sizeable in Latin America and will undoubtedly expand, it does not seem probable that this type of investment will be undertaken to any considerable extent in other underdeveloped areas. Even in Latin America it has gone to countries that, at this stage, can hardly be called underdeveloped. In sum, foreign private investment has made and will continue to make a highly important contribution to economic growth in a number of underdeveloped countries. It is a particularly fruitful type of investment because it customarily carries its own technical assistance. Countries seeking economic development and confronted with what at best will be a serious shortage of capital should encourage foreign investors to undertake as much of the task as they are willing. Even with the best efforts, of both advanced and underdeveloped countries to encourage foreign private investment, I do not think, however, that this source will account for more than a small part of the resources needed to put the underdeveloped world "over the hump." And even this part will be, geographically, unequally distributed.

This brings us, finally, to public and quasi-public grants and loans. There are many, both in the advanced and in the economically backward countries, who believe that without a very considerable expansion of this source of funds, sustained economic growth, along non-Communist lines will be, in a large part of the underdeveloped world, impossible. I am not here concerned with the prospects for these sources or with the conditions under which the prospects might be realized, having spoken my piece on this subject elsewhere.[15] I wish only to enlarge on the obvious; that is, insofar as these resources flow into development, they inevitably flow mainly through government channels.

I conclude then that both the technological and psychological requirements for development and the probable sources of funds indicate a dominant role for government. The technological influences stem from the significance for current economic growth of the transplantation of a capital intensive Western technology. The psychological or political influences spring, in large part, from currently held expectations regarding the rate and direction of growth. Undoubtedly these observations better characterize the situation in Southern Asia and the Middle East than in Latin America or Africa south of the Sahara. It does not follow, of course, that in Southern Asia and the Middle East government domination will bring about the achievement of self-sustaining growth. There is frequently a big gap between popular expectations and government action—and another large gap between public policy and what in fact happens. The really effective steps toward development, even in Southern Asia, may be taken in the private sector. And some countries may continue to stagnate. My central point is that the forces favoring government initiation and domination of the development process in the underdeveloped world are currently very strong.

III

These forces stem not only from the asserted need for government initiative in expanding the availability of resources but also from considerations having to do with the direction of resource use. A spring into sustained growth allegedly requires not only a big push but a careful planning of expanded resource use. Presumably this can only be undertaken by government. As I have already indicated, the arguments for the big push and for a substantial degree of government direction of investment are, to a considerable degree, overlapping arguments. To the extent that resource expansion takes the form of an extended public works progam, the case for planning in this area of investment is unarguable. Beyond this, extreme discontinuities in rapid developmental investment may create a presumption for some sort of public action to accelerate the capture of resulting potential external economies. But the current case for a directed breakthrough into sustained growth goes much further than this. Direction is necessary to bring about "balanced growth," to realize the full economies of scale, and to take account of the indirect effects of current investment on future savings, labor skills, and population growth. The case for control becomes then a fairly comprehensive attack on the free market as the primary director of resource use—at least in the early stages of development.

Indeed, it goes without saying, that the unregulated free market may not be a very effective allocator of economic resources, and there are reasons for believing that it may be less effective in the early period of development than at later stages. The classical demonstration of the merits of a "spontaneous order" achieved by unregulated market forces rests upon assumptions that are fairly unrealistic for any economy and markedly so in the case of most underdeveloped areas.

Indivisibilities in the factors of production may prevent certain installations or limit them to an uneconomic scale. If, however, the investor can be assured of simultaneous investment in facilities consuming his product, the prospects are more favorable. It is unlikely, however, the planners argue, that simultaneous expansion of complementary facilities will take place in the early stages of development without government direction and encouragement. According to Rosenstein-Rodan, "Complementarity of different industries provides the most important set of arguments in favor of large-scale planned industrialization."[16]

Such a planned development not only makes it possible to realize internal economies of scale in particular investments but also reduces the risk, and therefore, the cost of all installations. To the extent that such a reduction can be brought about, it represents a real external economy; but, say the planners, it is unlikely to be realized without a central direction of investment.

The construction of plants of optimum size in underdeveloped economies is rather likely to lead to monopoly. Certainly industrial concentration tends to be greater in backward than in advanced economies, at least in those industries in which Western techniques predominate. Until recently there was only one iron and steel making firm in India. Currently there is only one paper mill in Pakistan. But the classic arguments for the unregulated market assume the existence of effective competition. Insofar as monopoly and oligopoly are inevitably associated with the early stages of development, the case for government control or ownership is strengthened. One of the arguments advanced for government operated plants in Pakistan is the necessity of moderating, by public competition, the monopolistic pricing of private enterprise.

The direction of investment, moreover, can have a sizeable effect on the rate of increase and the quality of factors of production. Investment policy, warns Leibenstein, must take account not only of the magnitude of the output stream but "what happens to that output stream."[17] How is it likely to be distributed among capital goods accumulation, human investment, and luxury consumption? If industrialization tends to generate profits for reinvestment while investment in urban real estate generates incomes destined largely for luxury consumption, there is a *prima facie* case for directing investment into the former channel and out of the latter.

The direction of investment may also have a significant influence on the training of a labor force that then becomes available for other employment. In the minds of some students of development this argues for the introduction of techniques that are more capital intensive than existing factor proportions would appear to justify or than private enterprise would introduce. Mechanical techniques, it is suggested, perform a training function and exert a labor discipline than can stimulate development elsewhere in the economy.[18] These and other resultants of the direction of investment, however, are not likely to be taken into account by unregulated private enterprise.

Institutional obstacles and ignorance tend to immobilize the labor force in many underdeveloped areas—particularly in agriculture. Together with other influences in the cultural environment these immobilities may create a marked discrepancy between actual wage rates and what might be called the equilibrium wage rate. Some observers contend that in many underdeveloped areas the marginal productivity of agricultural labor is at, or close to, zero. If this is so, there is a case for putting this labor to work at any employment in which their product is greater than zero. But, since wage payments are necessarily at going rates, no employment having a product of less than these rates is within the possibility of private enterprise. Only government, it is said, can bring about a better distribution of such labor resources.

For these and other reasons, according to the planners, the unregulated market is incapable of accomplishing an allocation of resources conducive to rapid development. What is needed is the implementation of a strategy of development, a strategy that will take into account the various indirect effects of investment inevitably neglected in the private calculus. In the minds of some, the key note of this strategy is the notion of balanced growth. So far as I know, there is no generally accepted definition of balance, but the central emphasis is clearly on the complementarity of economic processes. A developmental strategy capable of taking account of these complementaries would presumably make it possible to realize not only important internal economies of scale but those external economies that are said to explain so large a part of Western economic progress. It is unnecessary here to subject this notion of balanced growth to critical analysis since my prime objective is rather to suggest the nature of the attack on the market as a satisfactory instrumentality for the direction of investment in underdeveloped economies. [19] The point is, that the type of balance sought would require a substantial degree of government direction.

The points that have been made in this attack on the market are, generally, well taken. The market is an imperfect instrument at best, and there appears to be good reason for believing that, in early stages of development, its malfunctioning is particularly evident. Indivisibilities in factor employment are probably more serious: the opportunities for capturing external economies are larger, the relevance of information signaled by the market is less, and the market imperfections greater than at later stages of development. The inter-industry relationships and the time horizon relevant to development that can come within the scope of a planning commission are much greater than the decisions a private enterprise would normally encompass. Yet the problems of information gathering that confront the planner, not to mention administrative and political difficulties, are enormous. I do not refer merely to the lack of statistical data, although that is characteristic of all underdeveloped countries, but also to the absence of procedures of estimating those economic relations which must be known if the planner is to correct the unregulated decisions of the market. The fact of the matter seems to be that the really good arguments for planning lie in the obvious inadequacies of the market, and the really good arguments for the market rest on the deficiencies of planning. As in some other fields of activity and of discourse, the best defence is the attack. In many underdeveloped countries the planners are clearly on the attack.

IV

As I have pointed out, it would be possible for government to exercise a large developmental role in expanding the supply of resources and directing their use, while leaving management substantially in private hands. Indeed this has been characteristic of development in certain areas. Puerto Rico has provided a considerable share of developmental capital and has exerted substantial influence on the direction of investment while leaving management pretty much to private enterprise. As the director of the Puerto Rican Industrial Development Corporation has said, in speaking of price setting and wage negotiations by government owned enterprises,

"You can take my word for it, that's one of the more difficult ways to meet a payroll."[20] In Pakistan several of the new industrial plants, constructed by the Pakistan Industrial Development Corporation, a government agency, have been put in the hands of private managing agencies. A number of governments embarking on industrialization have entered into contracts with foreign firms to undertake the management of new enterprises while training local replacements. Or, without undertaking a management contract, foreign firms have agreed to train technical and management personnel. Thus Pan American has a number of such arrangements designed to provide local government airlines with trained management and with skilled maintenance and flight personnel. Perhaps the largest training arrangement of this sort is the one designed to train several hundred management and engineering personnel for the new Indian steel mills.

These management and management-training arrangements are temporary, however; and for the most part, the local management personnel, once trained, will be in charge of publicly operated enterprises. Furthermore, it is argued that in the transfer of Western developed technology, so indispensable to the growth of backward areas, government rather than local private enterprise must play the dominant role. Thus on management grounds as well as on grounds of resource direction and expansion, the case is made for public rather than private initiative.

This case rests in part on a proposition of allegedly general applicability to all currently underdeveloped areas. It is said that whereas the development of the techniques and forms of organization that characterize an industrial economy may well have required a private initiative relatively unfettered by public controls, the transfer of the developed forms and techniques can be as well or better accomplished by government action. Thus Talcott Parsons comments, "In the case of the *original* development of industrialism, I have argued that it could not have occurred without the freeing of private enterprise from certain types of political control. In the present important case, on the other hand, I shall argue that political authority is usually a necessary agency and that, under certain conditions, far from obstructing, it is likely strongly to facilitate the process."[21]

And again, "It is only because the essential structure of modern industrialism has already been in existence in the Western world that political initiative has been able to take the main lead in its promotion elsewhere—starting with Japan and Soviet Russia."[22]

Lack of time prevents me from giving this thesis the attention it deserves. Let me say, however, that I agree with Parsons that "the balance between governmentally controlled and free-enterprise industry is to a far larger degree than is generally held a pragmatic question and not one of fundamental principles." [23] Or, to put this proposition in language I have used earlier, the optimal relation of government to business in the developmental process of a particular country is a relative matter. Among the factors to which it relates are the state of development in the rest of the world, the character of the country's government as shaped by its history, and the kind of private entrepreneurship that its culture is likely to produce.

Beyond this a few cautionary remarks would appear to be necessary. There is an unstated presumption in much of the writing on this subject that "industrialism" is a finished system that can, indifferently, be transferred to public or private hands for purposes of routine administration. In fact, "industrialism" embraces a set of rapidly changing techniques and administrative practices that are apt to evolve rather differently in private than in public hands. There is a further presumption that the methods developed in the West can be transferred without significant adaptation as "one man might wear another man's clothes," to borrow a phrase from Hagen. (He goes on to assert the contrary—perhaps a little over emphatically. [24])

The transferrability thesis, moreover, tends to treat the introduction of large-scale Western techniques not merely as an important element in, but the essence of, economic development. In fact, it is a relatively small part of what is needed in most underdeveloped areas to achieve sustained economic growth. This thesis also assumes that production with known techniques is the prime consideration. But government management may be able to handle this problem while failing miserably in the fields of selling, exporting, and product and process adaptation and improvement. Finally, there is a tendency to apply to all underdeveloped areas a proposition that, at best, is relevant, at this stage, to only a few.

Among countries in the present underdeveloped world, India and Pakistan appear to represent the closest fit to the model here suggested, but for rather special reasons. The development programs of both countries have emphasized rather strongly the installation of large-scale Western technology, and in both countries government is attempting to play the dominant role in the industrialization process. In neither country, but particularly in Pakistan, do there exist many private firms with experience in the administration of large-scale enterprise along Western lines. There are in India, of course, some large private enterprises, but even the largest managing agencies are typically family concerns, and they tend to be nepotistic to a remarkable degree. The firm is expected to take care of family obligations, and as one writer puts it, "the cost of hiring a brother is something like paying one's wife a salary."[25] The eagerness with which able young Indians and Pakistani seek employment in British, American, and other foreign firms is one indication of the obstacles to selection and promotion on the basis of merit that is found in local enterprises. The public service, on the other hand, thanks largely to a century-old British tradition, is a highly selective body of experienced men capable of attracting some of the best talent in the subcontinent. In both India and Pakistan the public service confronts problems of frightening magnitude in the management of industrial enterprises to which their governments have become committed. But, in considering the relative capacities of public and private administration in the two countries, it is rather easy to understand why government has assumed its role in the industrialization process.

Ataturk envisioned the same role for government in the economic development of Turkey, as did Reza Shah in Iran. In neither country was there a strong tradition of private enterprise. In Turkey the business classes were largely composed of Armenians and Greeks, and when they disappeared after World War I in the exchange of persons decreed by the Lausanne settlement, there were few nationals capable of taking their place. The industrialization that later formed an essential part of Ataturk's policy of Westernization, and which has been accelerated since World War II, became government dominated almost by default. The same considerations motivated governmental attempts at industrialization in Iran both before and since World War II. Unfortunately, neither Turkey nor Iran possessed a Civil Service of anything like the Indian competence.

In the rest of the underdeveloped world, however, there is no reason to suppose that, apart from the provision of economic overhead, governments will play anything like this dominant role in the managerial transfer of large-scale Western techniques and methods—at least in the near future. In the Latin American countries the tradition of private enterprise is much stronger and the establishment of foreign-owned branch plants will, in all probability, effectively supplement the domestic industrialization effort. In Southeast Asia, while there is little probability that local private enterprise will assume this role, there is likewise not much chance in the near future that governments will be able to do better.

I conclude then that in a few underdeveloped countries management considerations may favor an important participation by government in the introduction of large-scale techniques and organizations. This participation becomes possible mainly because the development of Western types of business organization has been away from the family-sized firm and toward a large-scale bureaucracy that, in some areas, comes closer to public administration than to the management practices characteristic of local private enterprises. Currently, however, these considerations seem applicable to only a few countries and, even in these, touch only a small part of the development problem.

V

In this chapter I have been more concerned with suggesting the nature of the case for extensive government participation in the initiation of development programs than with a balanced appraisal of possibilities of success. It is obvious that the case rests more strongly on the admitted deficiencies in the private sector in most underdeveloped countries than on any demonstrated capacity of government to make good these deficiencies. Essentially, the argument contends that the capital requirements of growth are unlikely to be met without heavy taxation and public borrowing from both domestic and foreign sources. A large-scale public investment program makes planning of some sort inevitable, and it may well be that a considerable extension of governmental direction of investment beyond the area of public works can usefully correct and supplement the admitted inadequacies of the market in early stages of development. Insofar as the importation of large-scale Western techniques is necessary to economic growth, the lack of capacity of domestic private enterprise may impose a part of this task on government. Above and beyond these "rational" considerations, moreover, there is a public pressure for government action that is all but irresistible.

The tasks imposed by these development requirements, however, are quite beyond the capacities of government in a number of underdeveloped countries. This is conspicuously so in some of the countries in Southeast Asia and the Middle East where certain of the basic pre-conditions of economic growth have not yet been met. As Cairncross puts it, a short-period take-off into economic growth is hardly compatible with "the replacement of one civilization by another."[26] In other countries, the task may not lie outside the capacity of government, though the problems are formidable. At the present time, India appears to offer the best possibilities for a government with this capacity.

Latin America is the only part of the underdeveloped world of which it can be said that certain countries are well along toward the achievement of sustained growth. The student of economic development interested in observing the growth process in motion is well advised to repair to Latin America. In Southeast Asia and the Middle East this process is not, as yet, well begun. Africa belongs to the future.

Chapter Four

Economic Planning in
South and Southeast Asia*

ECONOMIC PLANNING, as I explained in the last chapter, implies a substantial degree of centralization in policy making. While certain of the
policies embodied in a plan may look toward improving the climate for
private enterprise and perfecting the operation of relatively free markets,
thus moving in the direction of a decentralization of decision-making in
certain sectors of the economy, the so-called comprehensive plans now
common in the underdeveloped world conceive of government as holding
the main levers of development. It is not considered sufficient to rely, in
a Ricardian manner, on the reinvestment of private profits as the primary
source of capital formation. Expansion of capital resources requires the
creation of a budgetary surplus through taxation, public borrowing at
home and abroad, and, on occasion, savings forced by government-
generated inflation. It is maintained that the allocation of resources
through private response to market opportunities needs to be corrected
and supplemented by direct and indirect controls and by an expansion of
the public sector.

* These comments on planning in the Philippines, Indonesia, and Burma are based
largely on interviews with people inside and outside the government of those countries. The interviews were conducted during a tour of Southern Asia, financed by the
Ford Foundation, in the Spring of 1957. For the last five years, the author has been
an intermittent adviser to the National Planning Board of Pakistan and, during that
period, an interested observer of the planning process in India.

Consequently, planning, if it is to be something more than arbitrary, imposes some difficult tasks of data collection and analysis, lays a heavy burden on public administration, and requires an adept management of political forces and political interests. As I have emphasized, private enterprise in many underdeveloped areas seems a rather weak candidate for the assumption of heavy developmental responsibilities; and the free market as a central agency in the direction of resource use leaves much to be desired. But it remains to be seen how effectively governments can perform these tasks.

I

It is necessary in discussing planning in South and Southeast Asia to distinguish between planning as advice and planning as action: the word *versus* the deed. If we are to consider planning as an advisory function, we might first ask the question, how good is the advice and then examine how effectively the advice has been applied. In a number of Asian countries, however, it is unnecessary to ask how good is the advice because there is little discernible relation between what is contained in the x year plan and what in fact gets done. This may result from the fact that the plan as it emanates from the planning agency is never accepted as a program of action by political authority; or it may be that the plan is ratified by duly constituted authority, but because of various political pressures and inter-departmental rivalries, current developmental expenditures have a way of falling outside the plan; or it may be that the resources and requirements as envisaged by the plan are so remote from actual capabilities that the plan as a set of policy directives loses significance.

Almost all the countries of South and Southeast Asia have planning agencies, but in only a few can it be said that a planning process is in effective operation. In 1955, the Philippine Government reorganized the National Economic Council as its top economic policy-recommending agency. The Council, through its Office of National Planning, produced in late 1956, an impressive looking Five Year Economic and Social Development Program to cover the fiscal years 1957–61. This plan has never been put into effect as an operating program, however. The Philippine experience illustrates one set of difficulties facing the establishment of an effective planning process.

The Philippine National Economic Council includes an Office of National Planning, an Office of Statistical Co-ordination and Standards, and an Office of Foreign Aid Co-ordination. The function of the Office of National Planning is "to prepare and keep current a national plan for economic and social development." The reorganized Council is composed of a number of Cabinet officials and representatives of the Executive and a similar number of members of Congress, including certain representatives of the opposition parties. President Magsaysay failed to secure confirmation from the Philippine Senate of his original choice as Chairman of the Council; and the sugar interests, very strong in the Philippines, pressed upon him the appointment of a vigorous and articulate spokesman. The new Chairman formulated a development plan which was never published and announced a four-point program, the principal element in which was the proposal of four billion pesos of deficit financing of development. The President repudiated this program, and the Chairman resigned. His successor was widely considered to be a potential rival for the presidency. From that point on, the late President appears to have lost interest in the National Economic Council, having come to regard it as a body at least potentially opposed to his interest.

This development, however, did not prevent the formulation and publication of a Five Year Plan. This Plan proposed as a target a 6 percent per annum increase in national income, determined investment requirements through the calculation of sectoral capital-output ratios and, in general, exhibited the technical virtuosity we have come to associate with five-year plans. But it has remained an academic exercise.

Informed observers attribute the failure of the Philippine N.E.C., now generally admitted, to the mixed representation of congressional and executive interests. The congressional members, in particular those from opposition parties, sought to use their access to the Council's sources of information for political purposes, and the executive departments of government tended to limit their cooperation with the council for this and other reasons. On the other hand, it is pointed out that without congressional representation, it would be difficult for the President to carry through a plan he was willing to support. It is possible that a presidential system may not be very well adapted to effective planning. But the principal lesson of the Philippine experience seems to be that the first essential to effective planning in a democratic government is the existence of a disciplined political party under leadership strongly committed to economic development.

The failure of the Five Year Plan does not mean, of course, that there is no central direction of development in the Philippines. Planning, of a sort, goes on, but it is far removed from the Office of National Planning. As in most underdeveloped areas, a shortage of foreign exchange is one of the most serious limitations on economic growth. This means that whoever controls the use of foreign exchange has a very great influence on the direction and rate of development. Since this task in the Philippines has, since 1953, been entrusted to the Central Bank, and since the Central Bank is also in a position to ration credit to the very large number of government corporations that administer public development projects in the Philippines, this agency obviously is an important locus of economic control. But there are other important centers of power, and it is probably correct to say that, to date, the Philippines have not developed a governmental structure capable of initiating and carrying through a consistent strategy of development. Needless to say, this is not the same thing as saying that the Philippines are not in the process of economic development.

Indonesia also has planning machinery that, on paper, looks impressive. This machinery has, moreover, ground out a Five Year Plan to cover the years, 1956–60. The planning machinery consists of a National Planning Bureau which, in addition to planning, co-ordinates foreign economic assistance, and of a National Planning Board composed of six ministers with the Prime Minister as chairman and the Director of the Planning Bureau as secretary. The Planning Board, however, meets infrequently, if at all, and the planning staff, apart from its able director, appears to consist of twenty-five to thirty graduate students from the University of Indonesia assisted by a small group of technical advisers supplied by the United Nations. * The Plan consists essentially of an estimate of future government financial resources, a list of projects more or less related to expected revenues, and some projections of private investment that are admittedly guesswork.

There are many things wrong with the planning process in Indonesia. But perhaps the primary difficulty is the lack, in the central government, of any effective control over government expenditures and consequently over the supply of money. Until very recently the budgets of the government ministries were never completed until the end of the fiscal year, and their acceptance by Parliament was simply a recognition of what had been spent. The political organization of government, moreover, is such as to

* The Indonesian Parliament has recently (September 1958) "unanimously adopted a bill" establishing a new national planning council to "draft a national blue print for improving the living standard of the nation's 85,000,000 people as well as helping chart large-scale development projects. . . ."—*New York Times,* September 25, 1958.

make it relatively easy for any ministry to overspend such budget as it may have. The four principal parties are of nearly equal strength, and, apart from the Communist Party, their representation in the Cabinet has been roughly proportioned to their voting numbers. A minister who wants to spend more can usually force his will on the Finance Ministry by threatening to resign and thus upset the political balance. Even before the outbreak in Sumatra, it was not unknown for the Army to appear at the Treasury in force and successfully demand more money. This lack of budgetary control has permitted an expansion of government employees from roughly one hundred and forty thousand during the Dutch period to nearly one million at present.

Under these circumstances, control of the supply of money lies entirely outside the power of the Central Bank. Monetary policy in Indonesia is nominally determined by a Monetary Board consisting of the Minister of Finance, the Minister of Economic Affairs, and the Governor of the Central Bank, but the volume of bank loans is effectively determined by government requirements. In the spring of 1957, the government deficit was running at the rate of over two billion rupiahs per year, and it has, since then, substantially increased.

With the supply of money, the price level, the foreign exchange rate, government expenditures and government receipts out of control, the planning process encounters difficulties. Indonesia is one of those countries referred to by Singer, in which the establishment of the elaborate machinery of planning appears to be "absurdly irrelevant to real needs and possibilities."[1]

The Burmese experience with planned development is more promising than that of the Philippines or Indonesia, and I have little doubt that, in the course of time, the Burmese will possess an effective planning process. However, they still have a very long way to go. There is no doubt that planned development is a central objective of government in Burma, and the location and structure of the planning machinery reflects this interest. The Ministry of Planning, headed by the Prime Minister, includes, in addition to the planning staff, the Central Statistical Office, and is the operating center for all foreign contracts. The Planning Ministry plans for and recommends to the Economic and Social Board which formulates and implements policy. The Economic and Social Board, chaired by the Prime Minister and composed of the principal ministers concerned with economic affairs, takes its duties seriously. It meets eight or ten times a year for three- or four-hour sessions and devotes its attention to matters of current economic policy as well as to long-term decisions. Between meetings the Prime Minister and the Deputy Prime Minister are charged with implementing decisions.

A number of difficulties, however, clog the operations of this admirably designed piece of machinery. Central planning in Burma may be said to have been initiated by the government approval of the so-called Eight Year Plan largely prepared by a group of foreign engineers and economists in 1952. This Plan consisted of lists of desirable and feasible projects arranged in some order of priority, together with an estimate of financial resources likely to be available to government during the period 1952–60.[2] The government accepted this plan without much consideration of the rationale of the program and without providing any co-ordination of proposed expenditures in annual capital budgets. Moreover, the acceptance of the plan coincided with phenomenally high prices of rice immediately after the Korean War. And since the government rice-marketing agency continued during this period to acquire rice from producers at low prices, very large revenues became available for development. The combination of easy financing and lack of co-ordination led to the simultaneous initiation of a large number of development projects.

The price of rice fell in 1953, however, and as precipitously as it had previously risen—with disastrous results to public revenues and foreign exchange reserves. This necessitated sharp curtailment in various commitments and the abandonment of planned undertakings. Moreover, the disparate abilities of the various ministers managing economic ventures encouraged a highly uneven development: sugar mills were completed in advance of sugar cane production; power development has been disproportionate to the increase in power requirements, and—as elsewhere in Asia—the well-organized railway administration has shown an exceptional capacity to expand investment. Since 1953 the planning process in Burma has operated within the cramping confines of previous commitments and shrinking resources.

By now, however, the budget process has been strengthened and some measure of co-ordination accomplished. In 1957 a new four-year plan was prepared, though it has not yet been published. The technical personnel in the Planning Ministry complain that their role is pretty well limited to an annual assessment of resources. The various ministries present development projects relatively unsupported by analysis but heavily supported by political log-rolling. Indeed there does appear to be reason for thinking that, although the Government of Burma is strongly committed to planned development, there is little understanding within government circles of the nature of a development program. Commitments are still undertaken without an adequate investigation of alternatives and with little regard for considerations of consistency. Nor has the government ever made a serious attempt to enlist on a wide scale the support of the population for its development program.

These cursory remarks on planning experience in the Philippines, Indonesia, and Burma have, I hope, indicated some of the obstacles to effective planning. But before going on to the more successful experience in India and Pakistan, it may be useful to consider briefly some of the tests of an effective planning operation.

II

The "how-to-do-it" literature on planning usually presupposes one of a few objectives set by political authority and then concentrates on the problem of marshalling and allocating resources in such fashion as best to attain these objectives. The more optimistic practitioners conceive of planning as an exercise in operations research.[3]

The collection and analysis of data certainly is one important aspect of planning to which I shall return presently; but democratic planning, at least, takes place within a political environment that impinges on the process of decision-making at many points. And there are administrative considerations that the operations analysis frequently neglects.

It goes without saying that government planning will inevitably reflect the characteristics of the government doing the planning. A totalitarian government may be able single-mindedly to pursue an objective at variance with the desires of a majority of the population; a democratic government could not, for long, follow such a course of action. Planning in a highly centralized government is a different matter than in a loosely organized federal structure. The class composition of the population and divergent geographical interests will inevitably affect the character of the plan. All this does not mean, however, that democratic planning must inevitably be an economically irrational compromise of divergent political interests. But it does mean that the economic calculus operates within a fairly severe set of limitations. From the point of view of development it is the economics of the second best, the third best, and the fourth best, that is the real concern of the planner.

A single-minded concern with economic growth might dictate an exploitation of economic opportunities in the order of their prospective (social) rates of return, but political influences may urge a geographically "equitable" dispersion of public investment. According to Hirschman, a frittering away of public resources in small geographically distributed projects constitutes a more serious hazard to development than the large uneconomical steel plant or capital intensive heavy industry so frequently desired in underdeveloped areas.[4] Indian planning pays a great deal of attention to a "proper" distribution of public investment among the various states. And in Pakistan a politically acceptable allocation of development funds between the East and West wings is the first prerequisite of planning. This means that the development planner is concerned rather with problems of "sub-optimization" than with the *optimum optimorum* from the point of view of national development.

The economic calculus may indicate a thoroughgoing program of land reform as the most promising step toward economic development. But political realism intrudes to suggest a policy of the second best. The land reform program of the Congress Party in India has had to compromise with the differing political situations in the various states.[5] In East Pakistan, where the large landowners were mainly Hindu, land reform has been a much easier task than in West Pakistan where they are overwhelmingly Muslim.

Confronted with severely limited resources, the development planner may be tempted to pare down the allocation to social services and to primary education in favor of "productive" investment and technical training. But political influences are apt to set definite limits to action in these areas as in others.

The fact that political forces "choose" objectives other than that of maximizing the rate of economic growth does not, of course, make these choices irrational. Even from the point of view of economic growth an equitable geographical distribution of public funds may be desirable if such a distribution makes a large contribution to political stability, and there are national planning objectives apart from economic growth. Nor does the intrusion of these political considerations eliminate the necessity of economic calculation in planning, though it may sharply affect the focus and scope of these calculations. Nevertheless, it is possible for local and special political interests to exercise so intimate an influence on the process of decision-making as to defeat anything that might be called a national economic policy. This process of decision-making might or might not be called planning, but it would certainly not be national development planning.

The political process, moreover, impinges on planning not only by setting limits to economic calculation but in a more positive way. It is possible for a government strongly committed to economic development and enjoying the support of the governed to release and organize human effort that has not previously been put to effective use. Something like this was accomplished by the Japanese government in the late nineteenth century, and something like this may be in process of accomplishment in present-day India.

A partial economic view of the efficacy of a planning operation would probably take political objectives as given and treat as neutral the degree to which public support of these objectives had been enlisted. If so, the test of effective planning would turn exclusively on the technical competence with which the means to these ends are handled. From a broader point of view, however, we may appropriately consider whether the political support of the development program has succeeded, on the one hand, in enlisting to co-operation of the citizenry for a national development policy, and is sufficiently strong, on the other hand, to hold in check the pressure of special interests that demand a departure from this policy. As I stated earlier, the first essential to democratic planning is a disciplined political party under leadership strongly committed to economic development.

The economic calculus usually takes for granted the administrative competence needed for whatever use of resources is proposed or, if not, it treats the administrative problem largely as a set of manpower requirements that must be included in the plan. But a functioning economic enterprise is more than a collection of individuals with appropriate technical skills; and entrepreneurship, a scarce commodity in Asia, is not very amenable to rapid increase through the provision of formal training facilities. These considerations suggest that an effective planning operation needs to pay a good deal of attention to problems of governmental organization and that demonstrated entrepreneurial ability, wherever found, should be economically used. Governmental organization, public accounting and auditing practices, and civil service procedures, while admirably designed in a number of Asian countries for the conduct of "law-and-order" government, are not particularly well adapted to the effective management of economic enterprises or for the administration of detailed economic controls. A successful adaptation constitutes one of the most important and difficult problems confronting development planning. Of perhaps even greater importance is a due regard for the inevitable limitations of governmental capacity to manage and control.

Within the limits imposed by these political and administrative considerations, there still remains a large and important field for economic calculation. The problems of economic calculation center around considerations of efficiency and consistency. Efficiency, as we emphasized in the last chapter, is a slippery concept. It can be progressively broadened from a concept of market profitability to a concept of enterprise or industry costs per unit of output, then to a concept of enterprise or industry costs modified by external economies and diseconomies—by corrections for discrepancies between market and equilibrium prices, and by long-term calculations of the future uses of current incomes. The greater the departure from market profitability, the greater the difficulty of collecting the data relevant to an alternative concept of efficiency. And in most underdeveloped areas even the data necessary to a sensible appraisal of probable market profitability are frequently lacking. What is sometimes called the strategy of development is obviously closely related to the choice among alternative efficiency concepts.

The consistency problem is concerned with inter-industry relations in the economy. The expansion of any line of activity requires certain additional inputs and calls for the disposal of the additional outputs. If inputs and outputs are consistently related, both financially and physically, there will be no serious short-falls or production bottlenecks and no serious commodity surpluses or quantities of unused services or facilities. Considerations of consistency in planning embrace the private as well as the public sector of the economy. Expansion of investment in the public sector will inevitably have repercussions in the private sector, and unless these are fully taken into account, construction of publicly-owned facilities may be at the expense of underutilization of similar facilities in the private sector for want of needed raw materials or spare parts.

This all too superficial examination of some of the political, administrative, and economic aspects of planning may, nevertheless, be sufficient to suggest certain important considerations relating to the effectiveness of a planning operation. With these considerations in mind, I now turn to a brief discussion of planning in Pakistan and India.

III

Serious concern with development planning dates in India from 1950 and in Pakistan from 1953. The Indian Planning Commission has from the beginning occupied an important position in the governmental structure, and the preparation of the development program has been a primary concern of the Prime Minister and the Congress party. The National Planning Board in Pakistan was established as a temporary agency by executive order in 1953 and began to function in the spring of 1954. Although it was made a permanent agency in 1957, with the Prime Minister as chairman, it does not as yet have a firmly established position in the government hierarchy.* No leading political figure has espoused the cause of economic development in Pakistan, and no political party has made the promotion of development a central objective in its program. The importance of the political element in central economic planning is well illustrated by the difference in the character of the development programs in India and Pakistan.

The first Five Year Plan in India covered the period 1951–56, but it is probably fair to say that the significant impact of planning on economic development did not antedate the initiation of the Second Five Year Plan in 1956. During the first plan period the public sector program was, in the main, a public works program not very different from what it would have been had the plan and the planning commission not existed. Furthermore, what happened in the Indian economy during this period bore little if any relation to what was planned to happen. The modest proposals for public investment were not, in fact, attained. The private sector, on the other hand, far exceeded its projected rate of growth. And, because of a remarkable succession of favorable monsoons, the actual increase in national income, calculated at 18 percent, exceeded the planned increase of 15 percent. Unexpectedly favorable agriculture yields plus the fact that, at the start of the period, industrial facilities were extensively underutilized, produced a highly favorable ratio of investment to increased output during the plan period. This undoubtedly explains, in part, the serious underestimate of investment required to attain the objectives of the Second Five Year Plan.

Preparation for the second, and much enlarged, Five Year Plan cover-

---

* The chairmanship was shifted in 1958 to the Minister for Economic Affairs. The active director of the Planning Board is the Vice-Chairman, a high civil servant.

ing the period 1956–61, began some two years before the expiration of the first. The Planning Commission in India is composed of three full-time members and three part-time members, including the Ministers of Finance and Planning, and the Prime Minister. During the period of active preparation of the Second Plan, the Planning Commission met weekly, with the Prime Minister usually in attendance. The various proposals and issues involved in the projected Second Plan were discussed in the national and various state parliaments and were widely debated outside of government. Consequently, by the time the draft plan was ready for submission to Parliament considerable public awareness and enthusiasm and solid political support had been marshalled behind the government's development program. Although some high-level civil servants in New Delhi profess dissatisfaction with the extent of "grass-roots" understanding achieved by this process of public discussion, there is no doubt that, as compared with other non-Communist countries in Asia, India has been by far the most successful in enlisting public support for an economic development program.

The contrast with Pakistan, in this respect, is striking. Since there has been no general election in Pakistan since partition, there is no political party comparable to the Congress Party in India, which commands popular support and which might marshall such support behind a development program. The Muslim League, which occupied a similar position in the first few years after partition, has lost its commanding role. Since 1953, when the National Planning Board was first established on a temporary basis, there have been five Prime Ministers in Pakistan, each heading a precariously balanced group of ministers in danger of being supplanted at any moment by another group drawn from the same limited number of political leaders. Although the public sector program in the Pakistan Plan has been formulated in much the same way as in India—through the analysis and sifting of investment proposals coming from provincial governments and central ministries and agencies—and although the technical competence of this analysis has been at least as great as in India, the absence of organized political support on the one hand has evoked little popular understanding of, or enthusiasm for, the development program; yet, on the other hand, it has permitted, probably to a greater extent than in India, the acceptance of projects that have not been submitted to the planning process. In democratic planning there is no effective substitute for strong political leadership dedicated to the promotion of economic development.

IV

Administrative and management considerations impinge—or should impinge—on the planning process at all stages. A due regard for these considerations would limit the size of the public investment sector in a development program to dimensions capable of effective administration; it would counsel against the imposition of controls whose implementation lies outside the competence of existing public services; it would emphasize the importance of training programs and of necessary changes in government procedures. The administrative burden per unit of development expenditures obviously differs greatly among various sectors in the economy, and an effective planning process would take this into account. In certain sectors the shortage of trained personnel rather than lack of funds is the limiting factor to expansion. The effective management of particular enterprises requires decentralization of authority and responsibility, and this must be provided in a workable plan. In fact, a serious neglect of management considerations is characteristic of the planning process in many, if not most, underdeveloped countries.

As I mentioned earlier, India and Pakistan have inherited from the British public administrative services superior to those in most underdeveloped, and in some relatively advanced, countries. But the organization, procedures, and competence of these services inevitably reflects the requirements and purposes of British government in India. Apart from the administration of traditional public enterprises such as the railways, postal services, and irrigation works, these purposes concentrated strongly on revenue collection and the maintenance of law and order. Furthermore, it served the British interest to devise a system through which India could be governed by a relatively small group of highly trained men. Consequently, there is in both India and Pakistan a substantial degree of centralization of authority in the hands of relatively few civil servants trained in the strongly "generalist" tradition favored by the British. Effective management of the new enterprises in the public sector will clearly require a degree of decentralization of authority, a kind of professional skill, and management and accounting procedures, with which the traditional civil service is not familiar. The full record, then, on the success of the planning process in India and Pakistan, with their heavy emphasis on publicly-owned manufacturing enterprises, will not be available until more is known concerning the effectiveness with which these management problems are handled.

It is a truism that, in all countries, machines are easier to manage than men. This fact exercises its influence on planning in India and Pakistan in many ways, some inevitable and some probably representing the course of least resistance. It is easier, given the requisite skills, to secure a given output by administering a capital-intensive process than a labor-intensive process. Moreover, with an engineering orientation in management, it is probably more fun. A private entrepreneurial regard for costs tends to hold these preferences in check, but there is little check on the preferences of public management. A good deal of evidence supports the view that both in Pakistan and India public management shows little concern for the economies of labor-using techniques or for saving foreign exchange by the substitution, where possible, of local materials and labor.

These administrative considerations probably also strengthen somewhat the already strong ideological predilections for growth through large-scale industrialization. The administrative burden per unit of development expenditure appears to be much less in the building of large dams and the erection of steel mills than in schemes for increasing agricultural output in land already in use. Also, it appears to be easier to recruit administrative talent for the former than for the latter undertakings. Yet the agricultural situation in India is close to desperate, and in Pakistan it is indeed desperate.

Although nearly 60 percent of the labor force in India and nearly 70 percent in Pakistan are in agriculture, neither country, given ordinary weather conditions, can feed itself. Meanwhile the population in India is growing at the rate of 6 million a year, while Pakistan adds well over a million. The importation of foodstuffs already constitutes a serious drain on limited quantities of foreign exchange and, in the absence of improved agricultural yields, this drain will increase rapidly. In Pakistan the situation is particularly serious because of the progressive salting and waterlogging of irrigated areas in the Indus Valley. Unless corrected, this situation will worsen regardless of how the water dispute with India is settled. It is technically possible to bring these lands back into cultivation, but since thousands of agricultural units are affected, the solution presents a difficult administrative problem.

In both India and Pakistan, agricultural yields are among the lowest in the world. A substantial increase in these yields is the first essential to economic development. Without it, the increasing work force in the non-agricultural sectors cannot be fed and an adequate market for these non-agricultural products will not be created. The realization of such an increase under the conditions existing in India and Pakistan is much more a question of public administration than of financial resources. India is currently relying heavily on her Community Development and Pakistan on her Village Aid Program. But the best administrative talent available is required in both countries to handle these problems, and in neither country is this forthcoming.

Under effective planning the direction of investment always takes into account differences in administrative competence in different geographical areas and economic sectors. An even distribution of managerial competence throughout the sectors of public investment might justify one pattern of allocation, while the actual distribution calls for quite another. In both India and Pakistan the administrative competence of state and provincial governments differ widely, and so does the managerial capacity in different sectors of public investment. There are two ways of taking these differences into account: one is by allocating resources to the areas and agencies that can effectively use them; the other is by strengthening and improving management in the weak economic sectors and political units. The planning process cannot, however, go very far in the first direction without creating economic imbalance or without running into political limitations. The railway administrations in both India and Pakistan are long established and relatively efficient enterprises. This fact tends to influence the direction of investment to an extent that could probably not be justified by strict economic calculation. As I have pointed out, political considerations in Pakistan direct a relatively equal division of public development expenditures between the two provinces—regardless of the location of economic opportunities or administrative capacities. If this disparity in managerial competence among economic sectors and political units is not seriously to interfere with the best use of resources, a great deal of attention needs to be paid to the correcting of administrative deficiencies.

A foreign observer in India and Pakistan cannot fail to be impressed with the strong anti-business sentiment that permeates the civil service in both countries. Despite salutations to private enterprise in the Pakistan Five Year Plan, this is as true in Pakistan as in India; and the percentage of public to total investment tends, in fact, to be somewhat larger in the former than in the latter. There are, indeed, as I have frequently emphasized, many things to be said against private enterprise as an effective agent of economic development in the sub-continent. But when one contemplates the magnitude of the task that the planning process has assigned to government in both countries in relation to the demonstrated capacity of their public services to carry this load, one is entitled to doubts. Whatever has been or can be said of the private sector, its record to date, if the projections of the various plans are to be taken seriously, has been substantially better than that of the public sector.

V

Despite the limitations imposed by political and administrative considerations, there is still, in democratic planning, a role for economic calculation; though as I have emphasized, it is, in relation to a single-minded devotion to economic development, a calculus of the second, third, or fourth best. Such calculations focus primarily on questions of consistency and efficiency. Consistency implies a close relationship between requirements and availabilities, both physical and financial; a substantial part of the analysis in the Indian Second Five Year Plan and the Pakistan Five Year Plan is directed toward considerations of this sort. Efficiency, in a broad sense, is concerned with the way in which means are used to attain specified ends. If the ends are multiple, as they professedly are in the Indian and Pakistan Plans, a judgment on the efficiency with which the available means are used, would require knowledge of, or assumptions concerning, the rate at which attainment of one objective can be "traded off" for the attainment of another. Even if attention is focused exclusively on a single objective, say on the rate of growth of national income, efficiency, as I have emphasized earlier, is subject to a number of interpretations. It is much easier to see in the Pakistan Plan what type of efficiency concept shaped economic calculation than it is in the Indian Second Five Year Plan.

Enough of the experience of the plan periods has now unrolled in both countries to permit at least a tentative judgment on the probability of success in reaching the assigned targets. In both cases this judgment is, of necessity, decidedly adverse. The Pakistan Draft Plan, largely influenced by the example of India, set as a target an increase in national income of 20 percent. This was scaled down, on final publication of the Plan, to 15 percent. Pakistan will be fortunate to realize, during the last year of the Plan period, a national income 10 percent above that of 1955. Since population will have increased during this period by at least 7 percent, this means an increase in per capita real income of not more than one-half percent per annum. The Indian Second Five Year Plan set as its main target a 25 percent increase in national income. Although it is too early to say by how much the actual will fall short of the planned income, it seems probable that the short-fall will be substantial. Both plans clearly over-estimated the availability of domestic resources, and if more than the planned quantities of foreign exchange are available, it will be through decisions taken outside rather than inside the subcontinent.

Since planning is for the future, and the future is inevitably uncertain, a large discrepancy between actual and planned attainment is, in itself, no evidence of weakness in the planning process. This is particularly true in South Asia where, with agricultural output constituting more than half of national income, a good or bad monsoon can produce a sizeable positive or negative change in national income. Considering the character of Asian exports, foreign exchange earnings are likewise impossible to project with any accuracy. If we put aside the political and administrative aspects of planning and focus attention on the problem of economic calculation, relevant comment is pretty much limited to the care with which con-sistency considerations have been handled and to the reason or unreason of the development strategy that appears to be embodied in the plan.

Turning for the moment to the problem of consistency, it is clear by now that the plans of both countries seriously underestimated the rate of increase of governmental non-development expenditures with a result that, despite recent increases in taxation, tax contributions to development will be small or negative. It is also clear that in both plans the amount of deficit financing compatible with relative price stability was substantially overestimated. Beyond this there are certain evidences of inconsistency in the Indian Second Five Year Plan that are worthy of comment. In saying this, it should probably be emphasized that the problem of estimation in the Pakistan Plan is altogether much simpler. The magnitude of the Pakistan Plan in terms both of total and of public investment is roughly one-sixth that of the Indian. The Indian Plan furthermore proposes a far more ambitious change in the structure of the economy—a much larger step into the unknown. Finally, foreign government assistance accounts for a much larger share of development resources in Pakistan than in India. And, despite the vicissitudes of foreign aid programs in Congress, it has been easier during the last few years to predict dollar aid to Pakistan than to predict either domestic resource availability or foreign exchange earnings.

It is evident now that Indian planning has greatly underestimated the impact of large public spending on activity in the private sector. The results of this impact were already becoming clear during the last two years of the First Plan in the rapid expansion of private industrial output. This expansion was accelerated during the first year of the Second Plan by a sharp increase in the price level. In the atmosphere provided by expectations of large government spending, the outlook for private enterprise has been decidedly buoyant. Expansion of output and investment in the private sector, accompanied by a tardiness in the imposition of import controls that is difficult to understand, led to the severe foreign exchange crisis that had plagued the first two years of the Indian Second Plan. The investment-goods imports on private account absorbed during the first year the total amount projected for this purpose for the entire five-year period. The unexpected buoyancy of the private sector is also partly responsible for the failure of private savings to flow into government securities at anywhere near the expected rate. The failure of private savings and tax yields to provide the anticipated sums for public development expenditure led to an even greater than planned dependence on deficit financing. But despite this financing, government investment during the first two years of the Plan amounted to about 40 percent of total investment as compared to a planned figure of well over 50 percent.

It is also clear by now—and it should have been from the beginning—that the Second Five Year Plan very seriously underestimated the investment requirements for the planned production targets. The over-all capital-output ratio for the Plan works out at a figure of about 2.25; and there is little doubt that this extremely optimistic estimate of the productivity of investment was heavily influenced by the unusually favorable ratio attained during the first Plan. The utility of broad sectoral and over-all capital-output ratios for the calculation of investment requirements is highly suspect under any circumstances, and in the Indian case the lack of available data tends to make such calculations meaningless. [6] Even so the experience of other countries with a long history of development and better statistical data should have indicated that, for the composition of output projected by the Second Plan, the stated investment requirements were unreasonably low.

Since by now it is clear that Indian resources are inadequate to the attainment of the proposed targets, there has been some scaling down of objectives and an appeal for greatly expanded foreign assistance. The genesis of this appeal and the character of the response, which is apparently going to be generous, raises some serious questions both for underdeveloped countries and for those advanced countries that can normally be expected to be suppliers of capital. If development planning is to be undertaken not on the basis of a careful assessment of resources but rather on the selection of targets that run substantially beyond resources availability, any underdeveloped country can create an investment and foreign exchange crisis and hope for expanded foreign assistance. On the other hand, if development plans are carefully tailored to probable resources, the rate of growth of national income may be no more than sufficient to cover the needs of an expanding population with no improvement of living standards. This presents a dilemma that is likely to plague both the underdeveloped and the economically advanced world for many years to come.

*   *   *

As I have said, it is somewhat easier to discern the kind of efficiency calculations and strategy of development that underlies the Pakistan Plan than it is the Indian. Within the rather severe limitations imposed by political decisions, administrative considerations, and the difficulties of calculation, the investment strategy of the Pakistan Plan involves an attempt to equalize the social marginal productivity of investment in the different sectors.[7] With respect to power and irrigation, manufacturing, railway investment, and some other areas, where a rough calculation of returns and costs are conceivable, this means an arraying of projects in order of expected internal rates of return with the cut-off point for each sector determined by the prospective returns available in other sectors. In areas in which returns are not calculable, such as education, public health, and social welfare, the allocations to sectors were strongly influenced by historically determined ratios, but an attempt was made to compare the results expected to be achieved by each proposal with the results that might be achieved at similar cost by alternative proposals. These calculations were not very fancy. Apart from an early attempt to use "shadow" foreign exchange rates, which was no longer considered necessary after devaluation in 1955, no comparison of projected "actual" with projected "equilibrium" prices was attempted. Nor was any attention given to the "reinvestment" effects of projected income receipts. Consequently, the strategy of the Pakistan Plan is open to the charge that its "efficiency concept" was inadequate. It would, of course, be incumbent on a critic to produce an alternative operational notion of efficiency.

This description, however, is more applicable to the Plan as it emerged from the Planning Board and as approved by the National Economic Council, than to the public investment program as it is actually taking shape. The lack of political support, already mentioned, for *any* development program in Pakistan allowed the technical personnel of the Planning Board a somewhat freer hand than their counterparts in the Indian Planning Commission appear to have had. Political intervention came later, in the implementation of the Plan. A steel mill project, for example, which was given a low priority by the Planning Board, has since been accepted by government, largely because of the intervention of the able and energetic chairman of the Pakistan Industrial Development Corporation. A backward look after the expiration of the Plan period will probably have greater difficulty in discerning the development strategy of the public investment program than does an ex-ante approach.

Economic calculation seems to have had very little to do in shaping the development strategy of the Indian Second Five Year Plan. Both the national income and employment targets were formulated by high political authority, and the strong emphasis on heavy industry was initiated by the proposal of the Minister of Industries that India increase its finished steel capacity to six million tons. Although this initial iron and steel proposal was later scaled down, the very large program embodied in the Plan, together with the complementary expansion of railways, coal production, port facilities, and heavy engineering constitute the core of the development program. There appears to have been no analysis either inside or outside the Planning Commission of the question whether the proposed investment was a better or more efficient way of attaining the output and employment targets of the Plan than some alternative pattern of investment. Nor, outside the field of irrigation, is there any evidence that the calculation of prospective rates of return on proposed projects was considered to be a necessary function of the Planning Commission.

The aspects of the Indian Second Five Year Plan that have particularly interested economic observers have been the very large allocation of public resources to iron and steel and to heavy industry in general, and the limitation of factory output of certain articles, cotton textiles in particular, in favor of hand-loom production. There can be no doubt that the resource position of India is highly favorable to low-cost iron and steel production. The only legitimate doubt is whether, considering the limitation of Indian resources, so rapid an expansion is justified in the light of the prospective yields on other types of investment. Since, however, no calculation of alternative yields has been attempted, it is difficult to arrive at a firm judgment on this matter. The encouragement of hand-loom weaving represents a Ghandian influence that has little if any economic justification. [8]

It must be recognized, of course, that economic analysis as applied to such large structural changes as those embodied in the Second Five Year Plan has its distinct limitations. But surely analysis could have contributed more than it apparently has, to the strategy of Indian development.

VI

It is unclear at this moment of time whether the large governmental participation in Asian development programs is a temporary phenomenon associated with early stages of economic growth or whether it foreshadows a long-term "socialistic pattern of society." Certainly the former possibility cannot be dismissed. Government initiation of development in Japan was accompanied and followed by the rapid emergence of a business class that henceforth dominated and directed the course of economic growth. In a number of Asian countries local entrepreneurship is expanding, and in both India and Pakistan the vitality of the private sector of the economy is impressive. But too many diverse influences impinge on the path of development in this part of the world to permit more than a cautious recognition of this possibility.

* * *

In conclusion, let me say that neither this nor the preceding chapters have attempted to present a thesis either for or against government planning of economic development. A survey of Asian experience indicates how far even the most sophisticated of Asian democracies has to go before it can be said to have an effective planning process. But this in itself is not an argument against planning or against a very sizeable governmental participation in economic development. Democratic planning is something very new in the world, and, in any case, to arrive at a sensible judgment, one has also to consider the alternatives.

Notes

Chapter One

1 Lionel Robbins, *The Theory of Economic Policy* (London, 1952), p. 37.

2 D. R. Gadgil, *Economic Policy and Development* (Poona, India: Gokale Institute of Politics and Economics), No. 30, p. 84.

3 S. Kuznets, *Underdeveloped Countries and the Pre-Industrial Phase in the Advanced Countries* (Rome: United Nations, World Population Conference, 1954), V, 969.

4 See Harry T. Oshima, "Share of Government in Gross National Product for Various Countries," *The American Economic Review* (June, 1957), XXVII, 381.

5 International Bank for Reconstruction and Development, Combined Mexican Working Party, "The Economic Development of Mexico" (Baltimore, 1953), p. 13. The public share rose during the war period, declined to about 33 percent in 1946 and 1947, and rose again toward 50 percent in 1950 and subsequent years.

6 Eli F. Heckscher, *An Economic History of Sweden* (Cambridge, Mass.: 1954), p. 9. "The gap between policy and reality has usually been enormous. An efficient, honest, and incorruptible administration is a rare and recent historical phenomenon: even in large countries ruled by strong governments, economic statutes and laws have ever so often remained pious wishes exerting little or no effect on the course of economic development."

7 Justus M. Van der Kroef, "Economic Development in Indonesia: Some Social and Cultural Impediments," *Economic Development and Cultural Change* (January, 1956), p. 129.

8 W. H. Stead, *Fomento — The Economic Development of Puerto Rico* (Washington, D. C.: National Planning Association, 1958), p. 21.

9 Benjamin Higgins, "Economic Development in Underdeveloped Areas: Past and Present" (Center for International Studies, M.I.T., 1954 [mimeographed]).

10 In an illuminating article, "Economic Backwardness in Historical Perspective," Alexander Gerschenkron has discussed the relevance of "delayed industrialization" to the role of the state in promoting rapid development in the 1880's and 1890's in Russia; *The Progress of Underdeveloped Areas,* ed. Bert F. Horelitz (Chicago, 1952).

11 Bert F. Horelitz, "Patterns of Economic Growth," *Canadian Journal of Economics and Political Science* (November, 1955).

12 S. S. R. C. Conference on the State and Economic Growth, October 11–13, 1956; the papers presented at this conference are soon to be published.

13 See Simon Kuznets, "Economic Growth of Small Nations," ed. A. Bonné, *The Challenge of Development* (Jerusalem, 1958).

14 Abba P. Lerner, "Planning for Solvency and Development," paper presented at Conference on Planning for Development and Social Integration in Israel, Center for Middle Eastern Studies, Harvard, May 10 and 11, 1958.

15 Barbara Ward, "Development and Dependence in Emergent Africa"; to be published in *Public Policy,* Vol. IX, ed. C. J. Friedrich.

16 A. K. Cairncross, "Economic Development and the West," *Three Banks Review* (December, 1957).

Chapter Two

1 William Lockwood, "The Economic Development of Japan" (New York, 1954), p. 499.

2 See the phrase in Walt Rostow, "The Take-Off into Self-Sustained Growth," *Economic Journal* (March, 1956).

3 See John U. Nef, *Cultural Foundations of Industrial Civilization* (Cambridge, England, 1958). This series of lectures is a perceptive and erudite exposition of the view that the sources of the industrial revolution must be sought in the intellectual, spiritual, and aesthetic changes that took place in Europe during the prior two to three centuries, particularly in the period 1580–1660.

4 Everett E. Hagen, "An Analytical Model of the Transition to Economic Growth" (Center for International Studies, M.I.T., 1958 [mimeographed]. Mr. Hagen is directing a large study on the social and cultural pre-conditions of technological change.

5 Paul H. Baran, *On the Political Economy of Backwardness* (Manchester School: January, 1952). Baran has developed his thesis at greater length, but

in my view, much less effectively in his book, *The Political Economy of Growth* (New York, 1957).

6 Martin Bronfenbrenner, "The Appeal of Confiscation in Economic Development," *Economic Development and Cultural Change* (April, 1955).

7 *Op. cit.,* p. 71.

8 *Ibid.,* p. 78.

9 L. C. A. Knowles, *The Industrial and Commercial Revolutions in Great Britain During the Nineteenth Century* (London, 1921), p. 171.

10 John H. Clapham, *The Early Railway Age, 1820–1850* ("An Economic History of Modern Britain," Vol. I [Cambridge, England, 1930]), p. 413.

11 James L. Hughes and L. R. Klemm, *Progress of Education in the Country* (London, 1907), pp. 22, 23.

12 "The Distribution of the imaginable stock of institutions will in a very considerable degree differ according to the different circumstances of the several political communities. . . . In England abundance of useful things are done by individuals, which in other countries are done either by governments or not at all." Quoted by Lionel Robbins in "The Theory of Economic Policy," *op. cit.,* p. 39.

13 G. C. Allen, *A Short Economic History of Modern Japan; 1867–1937* (London, 1946), p. 30.

14 William W. Lockwood, *The Economic Development of Japan—Growth and Structural Change: 1868–1938* (Princeton, 1954), p. 507.

15 See Edwin P. Reubens, "Foreign Capital and Domestic Development in Japan" in *Economic Growth: Brazil, India, Japan* (ed. Kuznets).

16 Kuznets has assembled data on national income for fourteen countries, covering several decades. Japanese rates of growth both of national income and of per capita income were substantially higher than rates in other countries; Simon Kuznets, "Population, Income, and Capital," in "Economic Progress," ed. Leon H. Dupriez (Louvain, 1955).

17 See Edwin P. Reubens, *op. cit.,* p. 199.

18 *Ibid.*

19 See Joseph A. Schumpeter, *The Theory of Economic Development* (Cambridge: Harvard, 1935).

20 Carter Goodrich, "American Development Policy," The Case of Internal Improvements, 16 *Journal of Economic History,* 450.

21 Forest C. Hill, "Government Engineering Aid to Railroads Before the Civil War," XI, *Journal of Economic History,* 235 (1951), p. 239.

22 *Ibid.,* p. 235.

23 Louis Hartz, *Economic Policy and Democratic Thought: Pennsylvania, 1776–1860* (Cambridge, 1948), p. 292.

24 Vernon C. Fowke, "National Policy and Western Development in North America," 16 *Journal of Economic History,* 468.

25 Hartz, *op. cit.,* p. 293.

26 *Op. cit.*, p. 446.

27 H. W. Singer, "Economic Progress in Underdeveloped Areas," *Social Research* (March 1949), p. 4.

Chapter Three

1 K. E. Boulding, *The Organizational Revolution* (New York, 1953), p. xxix.

2 Michael Polanyi, *The Logic of Liberty* (Chicago, 1951), pp. 154–55.

3 Ludwig von Mises, *Die Gemeinwirtschaft* (Jena, 1932); see in particular Part II, Chap. 2.

4 *Op. cit.*, p. 122.

5 *Op. cit.*, p. 126; ". . . the reason being that the number of relations requiring adjustment per unit of time for the functioning of an economic system of *n* production units is *n* times greater than can be adjusted by sub-ordinating the units to a central authority" (p. 111).

6 Cf. Ely Deveons, *Planning in Practice: Essays in Aircraft Planning in War Time* (Cambridge, England, 1950); this is a highly realistic account of the merits and demerits of centralization, pp. 14–15. "This conflict between devolution and centralization appeared at every stage in the administrative hierarchy, At each level the co-ordinators regarded the plans of the individual sectors as futile and wasteful, because they took no account of what was happening elsewhere; and those in charge of the individual sectors regarded the plans of the co-ordinators as theoretical, academic, and unrelated to the real facts of the situation. . . ."

"Given the limitations of the human mind and capacity, this conflict was inevitable, and was the greatest obstacle to efficient aircraft planning. If the inevitability of this conflict is not recognized, planning becomes even more inefficient than it need be. For in such circumstances those who influence the planning machinery oscillate between a passion for decentralization, as a result of an exaggerated awareness of the inefficiencies of centralization; and a drive towards central co-ordination as a result of a terror of the illogicalities which emerge when important decisions are taken at the periphery."

7 C. A. R. Crosland, *The Future of Socialism* (London, 1956), p. 503. Crosland draws an interesting picture of the obstacles that a determined government effort to deal with the coal shortage, which he calls England's "greatest post-war threat," would encounter. "The Minister in charge might have to wage and win the following battles: (1) with Lord Citrine over the policy of the Central Electricity Authority; (2) with its own back benchers (not to mention the electorate) over raising the price of coal; (3) with the miners themselves and their M. P.'s when he urged the Coal Board substantially to raise the level of managerial salaries; (4) with the Treasury over discriminatory tax

concessions for the installation of fuel saving equipment; (5) with the Trade Unions (other than the Mine workers) in order to prevent an increase in miners' wages from being nullified by a corresponding rise in all other wages."

8 Max Milliken and W. W. Rostow, *The Objectives of U. S. Economic Assistance Programs* (Washington, D. C., 1957), p. 70.

9 P. N. Rosenstein-Rodan, "Notes on the Theory of the Big Push" (Center for International Studies, M.I.T., 1958 [mimeographed]).

10 Harvey Leibenstein, *Economic Backwardness and Economic Growth* (New York, 1957), pp. 94–95.

11 Everett E. Hagen, "Population and Economic Growth: A Non-Malthusian Model" (Center for International Studies, M.I.T., 1957 [mimeographed]).

12 W. W. Rostow, "The Take-Off into Self Sustained Growth," *Economic Journal* (March 1956), p. 25: "The take-off is defined as the interval during which the rate of investment increases in such a way that real output per capita rises and this initiated increase carries with it radical changes in production techniques and the disposition of income flows which perpetuate the new scale of investment and perpetuate thereby the rising trend in *per capita* output. Initial changes in method require that some group in the society have the will and the authority to install and diffuse new production techniques; and a perpetuation of the growth process requires that such a leading group expand in authority and that the society as a whole respond to the impulses set up by the initial changes, including the potentialities of external economies."

13 Hans W. Singer, "Problems of Industrialization of Underdeveloped Countries," ed. Dupriez, *Economic Progress, op. cit.* Singer develops this point but then goes on to say (p. 152): "Up to a certain point, it may have been an advantage to be a latecomer in economic development (e.g., the U. S.). By now it has clearly turned into a serious disadvantage." The underdeveloped countries, however, could hardly be at an absolute disadvantage, as compared with the initiators of industrial development, since they always have the alternative of devising techniques themselves, as their predecessors in development have done.

14 Allyn Young, "Increasing Returns and Economic Progress," *Economic Journal* (December, 1928).

15 Edward S. Mason, *Promoting Economic Development: the United States and Southern Asia* (Claremont, California, 1955).

16 Paul Rosenstein-Rodan, "Problems of Industrialization of Eastern and Southeastern Europe," *Economic Journal* (June–September, 1943), p. 205.

17 *Op. cit.,* p. 266.

18 See A. O. Hirschman, *American Economic Review* (September 1947), p. 563. "It is certainly true that an untrained labor force is likely to perform incomparably better in machine-paced operations, not so much because of a tendency toward slacking when the machine does not compel the work, as because machine-paced operations provide for steadiness of pace and regular

brief rest periods which the inexperienced self-paced worker has difficulty in observing."

19 See John Sheahan, "International Specialization and the Concept of Balanced Growth," *Quarterly Journal of Economics* (May 1958), p. 183, for a sober appraisal of the merits and demerits of this thesis.

20 Quoted by W. H. Stead, *Fomento—The Economic Development of Puerto Rico* (Washington, 1958).

21 Talcott Parsons, "Some Reflections on the Institutional Framework of Economic Development," ed. Bonné, *The Challenge of Development* (Jerusalem, 1958), p. 123.

22 *Op. cit.*, p. 110. Marion J. Levy has developed the same thesis; see his "Social Obstacles in Underdeveloped Areas" in *Capital Formation and Economic Growth* (National Bureau of Economic Research), p. 461: ". . . it is extremely unlikely that the highly modernized systems of the world today could have been developed indigenously on the basis of any systems other than ones that relied very heavily indeed on private individual operations, and that it is extremely unlikely that latecomers can carry out such development without relying very heavily on public operations."

23 *Ibid.*

24 Everett E. Hagen, "An Analytical Model of the Transition to Economic Growth," *op. cit.*, p. 70.

25 Charles A. Myers, *Labor Problems in the Industrialization of India* (Cambridge, 1958), p. 24.

26 A. K. Cairncross, "Economic Development and the West," *Three Banks Review* (December, 1957).

Chapter Four

1 H. W. Singer, "Economic Progress in Underdeveloped Areas," *Social Research* (March, 1949).

2 Knappen, Tippetts, Abbett, McCarthy, Engineers in Association with Pierce Management, Inc., and Robert R. Nathan Associates, Inc. *Economic and Engineering Development of Burma* (New York, 1953).

3 See Russell Ackoff, *Operations Research and National Planning* (Operations Research, August, 1957), and see also a critique by Charles Hitch, *Operations Research and National Planning—Dissent* (Operations Research, October, 1957). See also P. C. Mahalanobis, "The Approach of Operational Research to Planning in India," Sankhya, the *Indian Journal of Statistics* (December, 1955).

4 A. O. Hirschman, "Investment Policy and 'Dualism' in Underdeveloped Countries," *American Economic Review* (September, 1957), p. 551.

5 See Susanne H. Rudolph, "Some Aspects of Land Reform Policy" (Center for International Studies, M.I.T., 1957 [mimeographed]).

6 See D. R. Gadkil. "Prospects for the Second Five-Year Plan," *India Quarterly* (January–March, 1957), p. 11: "Was anything done in the formation of the Second Five-Year Plan which made a striking departure from the earlier practice? There were, no doubt, a number of papers produced by statisticians and some even by economists. It does not appear that they affected materially the structure of the Plan. Ultimately, given the policy biases which had been evolved, the Plan frame was based on common sense projections out of rough available data in various directions. It was always known that there had never been any real technical examination of the individual projections."

7 See David E. Bell, "Allocating Development Resources: Some Observations Based on Pakistan Experience"; to be published in Vol. IX of *Public Policy*, Yearbook of the Graduate School of Public Administration, Harvard University.

8 See Ragnar Nurkse, "Reflections on India's Development Plan," *Quarterly Journal of Economics* (May, 1957), p. 188.

Set in the Times Roman type designed by Mr. Stanley Morison for The Times *of London, printed letterpress on 60 pound Warren's No. 66 antique text, and bound in Strathmore's Beau Brilliant cover, this book was made well and speedily at the George Grady Press, New York City.*